CORNELL STUDIES IN ENGLISH

EDITED BY

VOLUME XXVII

SARA COLERIDGE AND HENRY REED

EDITED BY

Leslie Nathan Broughton

Coleridge, Sara (Coleridge)
"

SARA COLERIDGE AND HENRY REED

Reed's Memoir of Sara Coleridge
Her Letters to Reed, Including Her Comment on His Memoir of Gray
Her Marginalia in Henry Crabb Robinson's Copy of Wordsworth's Memoirs

EDITED BY
LESLIE NATHAN BROUGHTON
Professor of English in Cornell University

ITHACA, NEW YORK
CORNELL UNIVERSITY PRESS
LONDON: HUMPHREY MILFORD
OXFORD UNIVERSITY PRESS
1937

PRINTED IN THE UNITED STATES OF AMERICA

TO

VICTOR EMANUEL

WHOSE GENEROSITY AND INTEREST
HAVE MADE THIS WORK POSSIBLE

CONTENTS

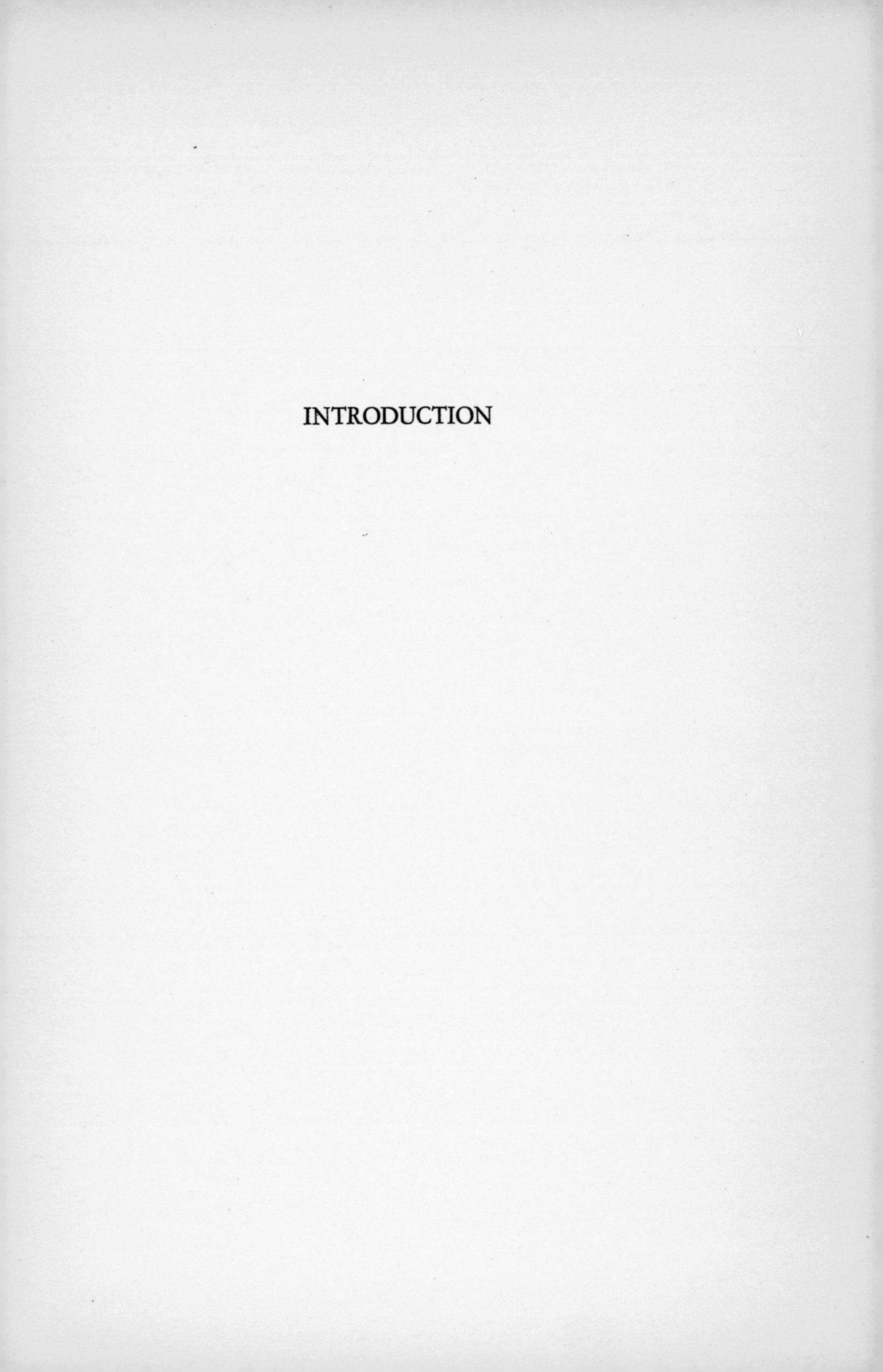

INTRODUCTION

INTRODUCTION

In the Library of the University of Pennsylvania there is a sonnet in manuscript by an unknown author, signed merely with the initial, W. According to a preliminary statement, the sonnet was suggested by Henry Reed's memoir of Mrs. Henry Nelson Coleridge. Although the sonnet itself has no great claim to literary merit, it is a genuine tribute both to the memoir and to its illustrious subject, and the topical aptness of the poem seems to make it a fit introduction to the former:

> Was not that Woman blest above her peers,
> Upon whose head worth, genius, beauty set
> Their triple crown,—whose infant glances met
> The starlike eyes of poets and of seers,—
> Whose soul, by wisdom nursed through ripening years,
> Grew to that high companionship; and yet
> Whose cheek with woman's smile was glad, with tears
> Of woman's gushing tenderness was wet?
> To whose young spirit, bending by the stream
> Fed from the crystal founts of ancient lore,
> Love came, to shed the glory of a dream
> O'er the clear waters and the solemn shore:
> Whose heart 'neath brows where early laurels gleam,
> Enshrined home's sacred joys. Could Earth give more?

The talented daughter of Samuel Taylor Coleridge is worthy of more attention than she has yet received. Unlike her brother Hartley, she inherited none of her father's waywardness and instability; like her brother Derwent, she displayed much of her father's strength, genius, and interests. To one thoroughly conversant with her powers and the charm of her personality, the highly laudatory tone of the sonnet above, of Henry Reed's memoir, and of Wordsworth's *The Triad* appears not at all extravagant. Hers were virtues not merely of character but of judgment: her opinions were sought and esteemed by many contemporary men of genius, and are still respected by able critics.

It is not the purpose of the editor here to attempt an introduction of Sara Coleridge, or even an appreciation of her work. That task he has appropriately left to that eminent and worthy American correspondent who induced her to write the series of letters, for the first time published in full in this volume, and who shared completely her confidence. In an unpublished fragment of a letter to Miss Fenwick, dated April 29, 1851, she remarks: "Henry Reed of Philadelphia is really an interesting correspondent." Apparently, however, she did not preserve his letters, as did Wordsworth; at least the editor has not discovered them. The reprinting of Reed's memoir, *The Daughter of Coleridge*, may, in some measure, compensate for the absence of his part in the correspondence. Though in some instances it may seem a bit extravagant, yet, for contemporary criticism, it has stood the test of time remarkably well. In 1854, when Professor Reed made his ill-fated trip to Europe, this memoir, which had but recently appeared, won for its author a most cordial reception by the Coleridge family.

The originals of the six letters in this volume are in the Wordsworth Collection of Cornell University. Nos. 1 and 3, the latter of which served as a postscript of No. 2, do not appear, even in part, in the *Memoir of Sara Coleridge* by her daughter. Excerpts from the others appear in that work, and a passage from No. 5 was published in the *Transactions of the Wordsworth Society*.[1] Extended or brief passages from them have appeared elsewhere. It is desirable and instructive, however, to see them exactly as written, with all the numerous digressions, abstruse theological discussions, and spirited comment on Ruskin, Aubrey de Vere, Christopher Wordsworth, and others, too personal for publication during the lifetime of those concerned. In these letters one learns with no little surprise and admiration that Mrs. Coleridge, hard pressed with social duties, disturbed by many interruptions, and without "time for any but brief letters," wrote a letter which occupies ten printed pages in this volume, and then added a postscript of two more pages before sending the letter;

[1]V, pp. 114–15.

and that later, in poor health and without leisure, she yet was able to write No. 5, the longest and best letter, filling sixteen printed pages. The long postscript to No. 6, written near the end of her life, when she had become an invalid and was in much pain, bears mute evidence of a richly stored and active mind. She surely respected her American correspondent, and her letters to him constitute a valuable chapter near the end of Sara Coleridge's biography.

The manuscript of Mrs. Coleridge's comment on the *Memoir of Gray* by Henry Reed, apparently an appendix to letter No. 4, is also in the Wordsworth Collection of Cornell University. The greater part but by no means all of this interesting commentary appeared in the *Memoir of Sara Coleridge* by her daughter. It is now first published as written, including the scrap (p. 85) penned on a small and separate piece of paper. For the convenience of the reader to whom Reed's *Memoir of Gray*, now rather rare, is not accessible, excerpts from that work appear as footnotes.

It was the last section of the present work, Sara Coleridge's *marginalia* in Henry Crabb Robinson's copy of the *Memoirs of William Wordsworth*, which suggested to the editor the combination of the four parts, forming as they do in spirit and purport an obvious unity. The editor purchased this particular copy of the *Memoirs* from the late Roger Ingpen in the summer of 1930. Mr. Ingpen had long retained the volumes in his possession in the hope of publishing the *marginalia*, which he considered sufficiently important, but business cares and failing health induced him to give up the project. The volumes bear the bookplate of Edwin Wilkins Field of Hampstead, who was Henry Crabb Robinson's intimate friend and executor. Mr. Ingpen probably obtained the volumes from the sale of the Field library or soon after. To the best of his knowledge, and so far as the editor has been able to discover, no part of the *marginalia* has hitherto appeared in print.

Sara Coleridge was disappointed with what she had written and almost wished it "rubbed out." Her comment, however, contains something of value, and, judging from the hints and abbreviated notes at the beginning and end of each volume, was intended to be much more elaborate. This work therefore is more or less a fragment, completed to some extent by part of letter 5, which its author wrote the day after she had finished reading and annotating the *Memoirs*. Low spirits due to rapidly failing strength and health no doubt tended to abbreviate the notes. Such as they are, no effort has been spared to reproduce them faithfully and minutely. It may be of interest to add that Henry Reed saw and read the *marginalia*. On June 21, 1854, he wrote home to Mrs. Reed: "Mr. Robinson showed me, at my request, the copy of the Memoirs of Wordsworth which Mrs. Sara Coleridge (as she told me in one of her letters) filled with her *marginalia*, and I spent half an hour reading them. . . . Among them I came across a note in which she made very friendly and complimentary mention of your husband, and another (tell Mr Yarnall) in which she spoke of him in like terms."[1]

Sara Coleridge's dissatisfaction with her *marginalia* was matched by her disappointment in the *Memoirs* which she annotated—that "compilation," as she described it, "of fragments and scraps of the great man's life of thought and action," a credit to the biographer's industry, but of no significance as a literary performance. The "compiler" was the Reverend Christopher Wordsworth, the son of the poet's youngest brother. For the author in his own field, theology, Mrs. Coleridge has respect, but here he knows next to nothing about the subject, and is out of sympathy with the great poet and his work. Was this criticism, we may ask, and much more equally derogatory, just to a work which generations of Wordsworth scholars have thought fundamental?

Christopher Wordsworth was a theologian of high rank, an able linguist, and a prolific scholar. We need but a glance at his bibliography to be impressed. Henry Reed met him in 1854 and has left an interesting description of his personality. "The Canon is a pale-faced, emaciated student—eminent for his

[1]L. N. Broughton. *Wordsworth & Reed*. Ithaca, N. Y., 1933, pp. 245–6.

labours as a minister, as well as preacher and theologian. He shows his hard work in his attenuated form, but has a peculiarly playful expression of countenance withal—an archness of manner which is an unwonted and most attractive accompaniment of the earnestness and solemnity of feeling, which are also perceptible both in manner and conversation. The higher manifestations of his character I had expected, but the attractiveness that accompanies them took me somewhat by surprise. . . . His look kindled with his eloquence in the pulpit. It was admirable pulpit oratory of a high order, animated in the delivery and impressive."[1]

Many of Dr. Wordsworth's personal comments and attempts at literary appreciation in the *Memoirs*, and his officious meddling with the text of *The Prelude* in the process of editing that work, bear witness that he was not qualified to become the biographer of his illustrious uncle. Unqualified, indeed, as he was in temperament and experience for compiling the *Memoirs*, "he would not," as he informs us, "of his own accord, have ventured on the task. . . . But a choice did not seem to be open to him. His revered Uncle, . . . was pleased to express a desire, and to commit that expression of his desire to writing, that he would prepare for publication any personal notices that might be thought requisite for the illustration of his Poems; and he afterwards dictated another document, intimating his hope that his surviving relatives and intimate friends would supply any materials in their possession that might be regarded as serviceable for this design."[2]

Since the task was not of his seeking and was thus injudiciously assigned, we must not censure the good Bishop too harshly if he did not perform his work in an altogether satisfactory manner. Within a month after the poet's death, he announced his project and advertised for materials in the English newspapers; and within a year (the Preface is dated April, 1851) he issued the two volumes of nearly a thousand pages, in addition to seeing *The Prelude* through the press in

[1]L. N. Broughton. *Wordsworth & Reed.* Ithaca, N. Y., 1933, p. 229.
[2]*Memoirs of William Wordsworth*, I, pp. 5–6.

1850, publishing two volumes of sermons, and attending to his heavy duties as a clergyman. We pause to reflect what might have been the result had Christopher Wordsworth been a Boswell and this task his supreme ambition instead of an added and rather unwelcome burden perfunctorily sustained. But Wordsworth in one of his poems had denounced personal talk and in one of his prose works deprecated Boswellism.

The Gentleman's Magazine held that the Editor had performed his task efficiently and according to the wishes of the poet. *The Quarterly Review* and *Fraser's Magazine* denounced most emphatically both the method and the content, but all three periodicals carried long and impressive reviews. That the work has merits and grave faults is admissable; that it has performed a useful service, no one can deny; and that it is less fundamental than formerly, since most of its material is presented in more scholarly form elsewhere, is quite obvious. It is not therefore the much desired definitive biography of Wordsworth, and such a biography, we must admit, is still wanting eighty-seven years after the poet's death.

In her criticisms of Wordsworth Sara Coleridge will find both support and opposition today. She believes his early works better than the later ones, though she evidently has nothing in mind prior to *Lyrical Ballads*, and does not consider that Wordsworth with the passing of years became more profound as a thinker, more exacting as an artist, spending much time in improving the careless work of his youth. She is severe, almost ungrateful, in her attack on *The Triad*. When she asserts that "it is just what he came into the poetical world to condemn, and both by practice and theory to supplant," she is thinking of the Preface to *Lyrical Ballads*, a work on his part avowedly an experiment which he gradually gave over. Three charming young ladies could hardly be complimented more cleverly and artistically. The subject did not lend itself to the treatment accorded *Intimations of Immortality*. The poem nevertheless contains much accurate character portrayal. Mrs. Coleridge's attitude toward *Lycidas* is equally unsympathetic and erroneous; indeed, it is almost as severe as that of Dr. Johnson. The pastoral monody, perhaps, still remains the most delicate and appropriate medium for expressing sorrow. Her estimate of *The Prelude* is in the main sound, although she knew the poem only superficially. The effective and brilliant poetry had by no means all been extracted and published previously, as she affirms. And Wordsworth was a bit more tolerant and fair to his contemporaries than she represents him to have been, at least with his pen. He allowed Byron, for instance, power, which is about all we can do for him now. Posterity has confirmed his opinion of Campbell. It was his privilege to dislike Carlyle and Goethe, shocked by the former's uncouth language and the latter's "inhuman sensuality." On the whole he made far fewer mistakes in contemporary criticism than we might expect. Mrs. Coleridge was much in doubt about the value of the poet's corrections of his poetry, and frequently so was he, but they were usually right.

There is no indication that Mrs. Coleridge thought of the ageing Wordsworth as declining in intellectual power. To her his character in old age was deep and strong, though greatly modified and adjusted from what it was in his early life. This view is particularly refreshing at a time when many are too prone to think of Wordsworth in his last years as a timid conservative in religion and politics and to proclaim his passing as a poet not later than 1815. Browning rashly wrote *The Lost Leader* because he was not fully informed. More recently a sensational and rapid manufacturer of biographies has written another Lost Leader, in commenting upon which a critic of sounder judgment has reminded us that it is not the leader that is lost but the followers. Were Browning living and writing of Wordsworth today, he would not portray him as a lost leader, but rather in the strains of *Rabbi Ben Ezra:*

> As it was better, youth
> Should strive, through acts uncouth,
> Toward making, than repose on aught found made:
> So, better age, exempt
> From strife, should know, than tempt
> Further.

We may agree or disagree with Mrs. Coleridge's views, but they will prove stimulating. They are the decisive and confident reflections and pronouncements of an able mind richly stored by study and experience, well worth knowing for her sake and for their bearing on literary history.

Some mention should be made of the author of the memoir and the correspondent to whom the letters here reproduced were addressed. Henry Reed (1808–1854), professor of rhetoric and English literature in the University of Pennsylvania from 1834 until his untimely death at sea in 1854, and also Vice-Provost of the same institution for the last nine years of his life, was a distinguished American gentleman and a productive scholar.[1] His secure place in the affections of Wordsworth of whom he was the first American editor, his recognized ability as a literary critic, his keen interest in matters of church and theology, his gentle, sympathetic nature deeply sensitive to the rights and feelings of others, and finally his desire and efforts to increase the fame in America of her illustrious father quite won the respect and friendship of Sara Coleridge. He was a correspondent with whom she had much in common and to whom she could write freely with full assurance of an appreciative understanding, and whose letters in reply, no doubt, were a source of pleasure and enlightenment to her.

The editor is indebted to the Reverend G. H. B. Coleridge for permission to publish the letters in this volume; to Mr. C. Seymour Thompson, Librarian of the University of Pennsylvania, for permission to use the sonnet at the beginning of this Introduction; to Professor Earl Leslie Griggs for help and encouragement; to the late Mr. Roger Ingpen for placing in his possession the *marginalia* in the *Memoirs of Wordsworth;* and to the Library of Cornell University for the privilege of publishing the Sara Coleridge letters in the Wordsworth Collection.

[1]L. N. Broughton. *Wordsworth & Reed.* Ithaca, N. Y., 1933, p. xiv.

I

THE DAUGHTER OF COLERIDGE

BY

PROFESSOR HENRY REED

The Literary World, Saturday, August 21, 1852, XI, 115-18

I

THE DAUGHTER OF COLERIDGE[1]

BY

PROFESSOR HENRY REED

The late London journals contained the following notice in the obituary list:

May 3 (1852). At 10 Chester Place, Regent's Park, Sara Coleridge, aged forty-nine years, only daughter of S. T. Coleridge, and widow of Henry Nelson Coleridge, Esq.

This brief and simple record is the announcement of the death of one, who may be described not only as a very gifted member of a gifted family, but in genius and acquirements one of the most remarkable women of our own or other times. Such was the modesty of her career of authorship and so little did she solicit public applause, that these words of strong eulogy may surprise many: but the friends who knew her and have studied her mind, her learning, and withal the beautiful feminineness of her character will recognize the praise as faithful and not fanciful. The highest critical authority in England, in an article written about two years since, speaking of the daughter of Coleridge, described her as "the inheritrix of her father's genius and almost rival of his attainments." To appreciate the panegyric implied in this comparison there is needed only the ready recollection of what were the poetic and philosophic powers of that father and what was the vast range of his erudition. The daughter's mind resembled the father's in its discursive character and in the well-constituted combination of the poetic and philosophic elements; with no self-considering economy of its strength and resources, it strove not for reputation, but, like the father's, with simple earnestness for the cause of truth in the large circuits of its thoughts in the regions of literature and art—of morals and

[1]A notice of the late Mrs. Henry Nelson Coleridge, written for *The Literary World*.

theology. The genius and learning which, if she had sought for fame, would soon have won it, were expended for the most part in editorial notes and prefaces and in familiar correspondence; and so varied were her writings and so rich in thought and in the accumulation of knowledge, that they may be compared to the conversation and "*marginalia*" of her father—distinguished by such difference as originality gives, and by the transfiguration, as it were, of womanly thought and feeling. In these resemblances much of hereditary influence may, of course, be traced, but in the educational formation of her mind and character, Mrs. Coleridge (as she remarked to a correspondent in this country) owed more to the influence of Wordsworth and her uncle, Southey.[1]

It is to be hoped that, in due season, a suitable biographical tribute will be rendered to the memory of this eminent lady; and we venture to add the hope that it will be the work of that sole surviving brother who found fit fraternal duty in the delicate task of telling with fidelity and with affection the story of the life of Hartley Coleridge. At present the object of the writer of this article is merely to throw together—without any pretension to method—some particulars respecting Mrs. Coleridge's character and writings, together with some of the references to her that have come under his observation.

It may be well to remark, in the first place, that Mrs. Coleridge's high intellectual powers were held in harmony with that feminine delicacy and gentleness, which sometimes are injured by pride or vanity attendant on the notoriety of authorship. Indeed a noticeable peculiarity of the story of her literary labors is that they were prompted, not so much—if at all—by ambition of authorship, as by some form of duty—filial for the most part, or maternal, which led to the publicity of print. If hereafter the narrative shall be given of the origin of each of her publications, it will be found that some moral motive was interwoven with it; and that in taking a public place in the company of authors, she preserved every

[1]*Cf.* Letter 5, p. 64, *infra*.

grace of female character in perfect completeness. It was a career of womanly authorship of surpassing dignity and beauty, disfigured by no mean motive or mannish temper. It was the same spirit, which kept her remarkable learning pure from all taint of pedantry, for she bore her varied attainments with the ease and grace with which a high-bred woman carries the customary accomplishments of female education. Well versed in theology, she discussed some of its most difficult questions, and, both in her printed writings and private correspondence, with a natural and unaffected ease, as if in simple unconsciousness of the possession of erudition lying beyond the range of women's studies, and indeed seldom attained by laymen; and so in her criticisms on art or on poetry —ancient as well as modern, there is the same graceful self-possession—the same unconsciousness of mere self—the tranquil and vigorous assertion of matured and well-reasoned opinion, ever coupled with such an unassuming womanly suavity, that manly scholarship, ever and anon remembering that it is a woman's work, stops to marvel at it. A great charm of all Mrs. Coleridge's writings lies in this: that you recognize not only the processes of a strong and clear-sighted intellect, but the full pulses of a woman's heart; they largely illustrate that unison and harmony of the intellectual and moral powers, wherein is to be found, we believe, one of the chief characteristics of genius.

It is not without interest to know that along with these eminent mental endowments the personal appearance of Mrs. Coleridge was very attractive. The loveliness of her girlhood caught the sense of beauty in an artist's eye; that accomplished painter, the late William Collins (distinguished chiefly as a landscape-painter), writing to Washington Allston in 1818, said: "Coleridge's elegant daughter, Sara, I have made a painting of. She is a most interesting creature, about fifteen years of age." The memoir of Collins gives also a characteristic criticism by Coleridge himself on this picture of his daughter; in a letter to the painter he says: "Your picture of Sara Coleridge has quite haunted my eye ever since. Taken as a mere fancy-piece, it is long since I have met with a work of art that has so much delighted me. If I described it as a union of simplicity with refinement, I should still be dissatisfied with the description—for refinement seems to me to express an after-act, a something superinduced. Natural *fineness* would be more appropriate. Your landscape, too, is as exquisite in its correspondence with the figure as it is delightful to the eye in itself."

Some years later, when the child's beauty had ripened into the developed beauty of thoughtful womanhood, another artist, using the pictorial power of words and verse, instead of the pencil, portrayed both the character and the appearance of Sara Coleridge. I refer to that poem of Wordsworth's—"*The Triad*," in which he has described the eldest daughter of Southey—his own, only daughter (her whose death was the grief of his old age)—and the only daughter of Coleridge.[1] The passage descriptive of the last is as follows:—

"Last of the Three, though eldest born,
Reveal thyself, like pensive morn
Touched by the skylark's earliest note,
Ere humbler gladness be afloat.
But whether in the semblance drest
Of Dawn—or Eve, fair vision of the west,
Come with each anxious hope subdued
By woman's gentle fortitude,
Each grief, through meekness, settling into rest.
—Or I would hail thee when some high-wrought page
Of a closed volume lingering in thy hand
Has raised thy spirit to a peaceful stand
Among the glories of a happier age."
Her brow hath opened on me—see it there,
Brightening the umbrage of her hair;
So gleams the crescent moon, that loves
To be descried through shady groves.
Tenderest bloom is on her cheek;
Wish not for a richer streak;
Nor dread the depth of meditative eye;
But let thy love, upon that azure field

[1]For Sara Coleridge's estimate of *The Triad*, see Letter 5, pp. 68, 70, infra.

Of thoughtfulness and beauty, yield
Its homage offered up in purity.
What wouldst thou more? In sunny glade,
Or under leaves of thickest shade,
Was such a stillness e'er diffused
Since earth grew calm while angels mused?
Softly she treads, as if her foot were loth
To crush the mountain dew-drops—soon to melt
On the flower's breast; as if she felt
That flowers themselves, whate'er their hue,
With all their fragrance, all their glistening,
Call to the heart for inward listening—
And though for bridal-wreaths and tokens true
Welcomed wisely; though a growth
Which the careless shepherd sleeps on,
As fitly spring from turf the mourner weeps on—
And without wrong are cropped the marble tomb to strew.

This is exquisite poetic painting—the imaginative portraiture of the finest feminine beauty, wherein are visible, deep meditativeness and the tenderest feeling.

The childhood and early womanhood of Sara Coleridge were spent under the generous guardianship of her uncle, Southey, in whose house at Keswick she, with her mother and brothers had a happy home for many years. During that period she also enjoyed the fatherly intimacy of Wordsworth, and very often was his companion in long rambles through the beautiful region where the poet dwelt—listening to his sage discourse with the earnest ear of thoughtful youth—listening (as she described it after the poet's death), not to record or even to remember, but for delight and admiration.[1] Under such propitious guidance, or in the joyous fellowship of her brothers or of her sisterlike cousins, did she learn to hold communion with nature, and thus was her poetic soul strengthened. In after years in dedicating to Wordsworth her edition of the "*Biographia Literaria*," fitly and with feeling did she subscribe herself—"With deep affection, admiration, and respect, your child in heart, and faithful friend, Sara Coleridge." Such, for many of the most susceptible years

[1] *Cf.* Letter 5, p. 63, *infra*.

of her life was the outdoor existence of this child of genius, and with it were combined the finest opportunities for literary culture, for her home was the house of Southey—a house of books—the laboratory of one of the most industrious and comprehensive students of the age. Never, perhaps, were such opportunities given for the formation of a woman's mind and character, and never were privileges more happily improved. The influence of her father's mind—other than that which was hereditary transmission—belonged to later years.

Miss Coleridge's first literary production was during her Keswick residence, and had its origin manifestly in connexion with some of Southey's labors: it began probably in affectionate assistance given to him, while engaged on his great South America history.[1] In 1822 there issued from the London press a work in three octavo volumes, entitled, "*An Account of the Abipones, an Equestrian people of Paraguay. From the Latin of Martin Dobrizhoffer, 18 years a Missionary in that country*." No name of translator appears, and a brief and modest preface gives not the least clue to it: even now in catalogues the work is frequently ascribed to Southey. At the time of the publication Miss Coleridge was just twenty years of age, and therefore this elaborate toil of translation must have been achieved before she had reached the years of womanhood. The stout-hearted perseverance needed for such a task is quite as remarkable as the scholarship in a young person. The modesty which marked the manner in which the work was put before the public seems to have continued in after years, for in none of her writings or letters, as far as I am aware, did she think it worth while to set forth her claim to the nameless translation.

Coleridge himself spoke of it with fond and just admiration, when in 1832 he said,—"My dear daughter's translation of this book (Dobrizhoffer's) is, in my judgment, unsurpassed for pure mother English by anything I have read for a long time."—("Table Talk," vol. ii., p. 81). Southey in his "Tale of Paraguay," which was suggested by the missionary's

[1] *History of Brazil*, in 3 Parts. 1810–1819.

narrative, paid to the translator a tribute so delicate, and so controlled, perhaps, by a sense of his young kinswoman's modesty, that one needs be in the secret to know for whom it is meant. It is in the stanza, which mentions Dobrizhoffer's forgetfulness of his native speech during his long missionary expatriation, and alludes to the favor shown him by the Empress Maria Theresa:—

> But of his native speech, because well-nigh
> Disuse in him forgetfulness had wrought,
> In Latin he composed his history;
> A garrulous but a lively tale and fraught
> With matter of delight and food for thought.
> And if he could in Merlin's glass have seen
> By whom his tomes to speak our tongue were taught,
> The old man would have felt as pleased, I ween,
> As when he won the ear of that great Empress Queen.
>
> *Canto III., stanz. 16.*

Charles Lamb, in an epistolary strain eminently characteristic, echoes the praise bestowed upon his friend's child and her rare achievement. Writing to Southey in 1825, in acknowledgment of a presentation copy of the "Tale of Paraguay," he says:—"The compliment to the translatress is daintily conceived. Nothing is choicer in that sort of writing than to bring in some remote impossible parallel—as between a great empress and the inobtrusive quiet soul, who digged her noiseless way so perseveringly through that rugged Paraguay mine. How she Dobrizhoffered it all out, puzzles my slender Latinity to conjecture."—(Talfourd's Letters of Charles Lamb, vol. ii., p. 189).

In 1829 Miss Coleridge was married to her cousin, Henry Nelson Coleridge, a barrister, and brother to Mr. Justice Coleridge, of the court of the Queen's Bench.[1] This event is

[1]The name of Sir John Taylor Coleridge should not be mentioned without the recollection that he was the "John Coleridge" of Southey's letters, and the successor of Gifford in the editorship of the Quarterly Review—of whom Southey writing to his American friend, Mr. Ticknor, in 1824, said—"Under John Coleridge's management there will be an end to the mischievous language concerning your country, . . . and henceforth that journal will do all in its power towards establishing that feeling which ought to exist between the two nations."—*Life &c. of Southey*, Vol. v. p. 194. [H. Reed's note.]

thus mentioned by Mr. Cuthbert Southey in the biography of his father (vol. vi. p. 72):—"The autumn of the year (1829) was marked by a great change in the household at Greta Hall. From the time of my father's first settling at Keswick, where, it will be remembered, he found Mr. and Mrs. Coleridge residing, she and her only daughter had formed part of the family circle, and now the latter was to change, not her name (for she was about to marry her cousin, the late Henry Nelson Coleridge), but her state and residence; and Mrs. Coleridge was about to take up her permanent residence with them. This, of course, was like parting with a sister."

This was the beginning of a married life, which lasted about thirteen years, until her widowhood. In some lines composed by her brother Hartley—dated January, 1843, and entitled "On the Death of Henry Nelson Coleridge"—in the following passage the poet's vision is turned in retrospect to his sister as a bride; and the beauty of her character—at once so gentle, and so mighty in the strength of its affections—is impressively portrayed:—

My sister loved him well!
She was a maid (alas! a widow now)
Not easily beguiled by loving words,
Nor quick to love; but when she loved, the fate
Of her affection was a stern religion,
Admitting nought less holy than itself.
Seven years of patience, and a late consent
Won for the pair their all of hope. I saw
My sweetest sister in her honeymoon,
And then she was so pensive and so meek,
That now I know there was an angel with her
That cried Beware!

The same poem contains this picture of her as a wife and mother:—

But he is gone, and all
The fondest passages of wedded life
And mutual fondling of their progeny,
And hopes together felt, and prayers when both
Blended their precious incenses, and the wish

That they together might behold the growth
And early fruit, most holy and approved,
Of their two darlings, sinks in voiceless night,
And is no more.
—*The Poems of Hartley Coleridge*, vol. ii. p. 178.

The married life of Mrs. Coleridge (if it be not intrusive to make the comment) was rich in the best elements of conjugal happiness: wedded to a gentleman of high moral worth, and of fine mind and scholarship—one who blended literature with his professional pursuits—she was not exposed to the perils of intellectual superiority. The marriage was blest with the birth of two children—a son and daughter—and the mother was too wise and gentle "to permit" (to borrow a phrase of her own, elsewhere applied) "the interests of intellectual pursuit to override those of the affections." The married life of Mrs. Coleridge was indeed exemplary and admirable, especially in this, that no sense of endowment of genius, or of learning, or of conversational and epistolary talent—no ambition of authorship or of distinction in the cultivated society she was familiar with in the metropolis—tempted her away from the paths of domestic life, wherein she found her duty and delight.

It was in such duty that Mrs. Coleridge's next publication had its origin. When her first work appeared in print, a maidenly modesty had kept her name in seclusion, and the simple little volume entitled, "*Pretty Lessons for Little Children*," was her first acknowledged act of authorship: this was characteristic; it was a mother's work which might be avowed with matronly modesty, and it shows to what humble service genius and high scholarship can gracefully descend. The volume, which has gone through several editions, consists of short pieces of poetry addressed to her son and daughter, partly for moral guidance, and partly for instruction in the Latin vocabulary and other elementary subjects. It is interesting to trace the fruits of the mother's zeal in the recent academic success of the son, who within the last few weeks has gained the highest honors in the University of Oxford—the name of Herbert Coleridge appearing as that of what is styled "a double first-class man,"—the highest rank of scholarship, both in classics and the mathematical sciences. It is sad to observe that the mother did not live to enjoy this recompense of a mother's care and promise of the son's future reputation; his Oxford honors were conferred about a month after her death.[1]

In 1837, Mrs. Coleridge published the fairy tale, "*Phantasmion*," of which the 'Quarterly Review' said,—"This beautiful romance is not a poem, but it is poetry from beginning to end, and has many poems within it. It is one of a race that has particularly suffered under the assaults of political economy and useful knowledge;—a Fairy Tale, the last, we suppose. that will ever be written in England, and unique in its kind. It is neither German nor French. It is what it is—pure as a crystal in diction, tinted like an opal with the hues of an everspringing sunlit fancy." And speaking of the fine metrical skill shown in one of the poems, the reviewer remarks, "These surely are lines which would have pleased the ear of Collins—or of *the* Coleridge." Article on "British Poetesses," Vol. 67, p. 411.

The death of Coleridge, in 1834, brought to his daughter a new set of literary duties, first shared with her husband, and then fulfilled by herself alone. The filial work occupied her whole authorship during the remainder of her life,—though much was done, which, it is hoped, will appear in the form of literary remains. Her husband was Coleridge's literary executor, to whom was committed the delicate trust of collecting and arranging for publication the scattered remains of that remarkable mind. Mr. H. N. Coleridge was, however, not only a man of letters and an author, but was occupied in a responsible and laborious profession; and it is reasonable to suppose valuable assistance was given to him by his wife, in the compilation of her father's literary remains, and in the editing of his works. During the decline of her husband's

[1]Herbert Coleridge subsequently became the first editor of N. E. D.

health, she was his helpmate also in his professional labours; and when it is mentioned that she was his amanuensis in copying papers for him as a chancery-barrister, it will be seen that her pen, fit as it was for creative or poetic service, was ready, for her husband's help, to do the mechanical drudgery of the most technical and unattractive copying.

The last ten years of Mrs. Coleridge's life were years of widowhood; for her marriage vow was such as, in Spenser's phrase, "would endless matrimony make," and when her wedded happiness on earth was over, it left sorrowing memories of the past, and Christian hope of its restoration in the life to come. To this subject I have found allusion made by Mrs. Coleridge, once, and once only, and then with a delicacy and depth of emotion very expressive in its reserve, and characteristic of a nature in which the powers of thought and the susceptibilities of affection were so well adjusted. In a soul so constituted, the memory of the dead husband, and all the feelings which clung to it, were things too sacred for any sentimental soliciting of sympathy; they belonged to the silence of self-communing thought. The passage referred to is in one of the notes to her edition of the *Biographia Literaria*, in which she replies to some remarks of Mr. Dequincey's [*sic*] on the infelicity of the marriages of men of letters, and his sarcastic comment on the happy phrase—"social silence"—which had been used by Coleridge. The whole note is very interesting, and in Mrs. Coleridge's best vein, but the sentences which, for my present purpose, I must tear from their context, are as follows:

> On the domestic part of the subject, Mr. Dequincey [*sic*] expresses opinions rather different from those which my experience has led me to form; I pity the man who cannot enter into the pleasure of "social silence," and finds nothing in Mr. Coleridge's description of a literary man's evening but a theme of sarcasm. . . . Somewhere else Mr. Dequincey eloquently declares that, "every man who has once dwelt with passionate love on the fair face of some female companion through life, must have commended and adjured all-conquering Time, there at least, and upon that one tablet of his adoration,
>
> "To write no wrinkle with his antique hand."

There is a tenderness of feeling in this, but a still better feeling is displayed in strains like those of Mr. Wordsworth, which, not content with drily exposing the emptiness of any such "rebellion against the laws that season all things for the inexorable grave," supply reflections whereby, even in this life, Time may be set at defiance,—grace and loveliness may be discerned in every age, as long as the body continues to be a translucent tenement of the mind. But without contending any longer on behalf of those whose charms of *youth* are departed or transmuted, I do maintain, that a wife, whether young or old, may pass her evenings most happily in the presence of her husband, occupied herself, and conscious that he is still better occupied, though he may but speak with her, and cast his eyes upon her from time to time; that such evenings may be looked forward to with great desire, and deeply regretted when they are passed away for ever.—Appendix, Note O.

The literary labors of Mrs. Coleridge, during the ten years of her widowed life, were devoted to one pursuit—the completion of what her husband had begun—the editorial care of her father's writings, and the guardianship of his character as a poet, a critic, and most of all, as a Christian philosopher. These labors had a moral impulse in the genial sense of duty to the memory of both her father and her husband. It was fit filial and conjugal work; and intellectually it gave full scope to her genius and learning in following the footsteps of her father. There was, too, extraordinary unselfishness in it; for the work was necessarily immethodical and desultory; and thus there have been expended, in the fragmentary form of notes, and prefaces, and appendixes, an amount of original thought and an affluence of learning, which, differently and more prominently presented would have made her famous. But it was her father's fame, and not her own that was foremost in her thoughts; and it is this that puts her character in such fine contrast with the self-considering temper of common authorship. There is not one woman in a thousand, nor one man in ten thousand, who would be content to be thus prodigal of the means of celebrity. Mrs. Coleridge's editorship comprehended first, the 'Biographia Literaria' (which her husband had commenced,) then the 'Aids to Reflection,' and afterwards the 'Notes on Shakespeare and the Dramatists';

the 'Essays on his own Times', and other of her father's works. In her notes and other additions are proved respectively her powers of criticism and of reasoning, especially in theology. The 'Essay on Rationalism,' involving a discussion of the subject of Baptismal Regeneration, though in form simply a prefatory note to the 'Aids to Reflection,' is a treatise which, as the composition of a woman, may be pronounced unparalleled: there is no instance in which a woman has travelled so far and so firmly into the region of severe study or sustained such continuous processes of argumentation,—the subject demanding too extensive research in doctrinal theology. A beautiful proof of her genius and of her varied power, both as a writer of prose and as a poet, occurs in one of the notes, when, in answer to a theological dogma, in support of which a passage from 'The Christian Year' had been quoted, she first treats the truth she is contending for as a question of strict logic and theological authority, and then turning, as it were, to the great living master of sacred song, who had been cited, she appeals to him in a strain of verse which is comparable to his own—as song in the service of the highest truth.

The most attractive of Mrs. Coleridge's writings, in connexion with her editorial labors, will be found in her criticisms—especially those on poetry. Her comment on "The Song at the Feast of Brougham Castle" may be mentioned as one of the choicest pieces of criticism in the language. In comment—at once imaginative and analytical (and such must be the best criticism on art in any of its forms)—upon poetry, she possessed much of her father's peculiar ability, and some powers, in which, perhaps, she excelled him. One of her most remarkable editorial enterprises was the work to which she gave the title of "Essays on his own Times, by S. T. Coleridge." This required her to identify and collect her father's contributions to the London newspaper press during some of the early years of this century—a task of peculiar difficulty to which no hand but one strengthened by filial zeal such as hers would have been equal. This undertaking carried Mrs. Coleridge into the sphere of political history; and the original introductory "Sections" are no less noticeable than her writings on literature, art, or theology. The two chapters devoted to a comparison of British and American civilization contain the most judicious and impartial discussion of the social and intellectual condition of the two countries, which has been written. In the last letter which she wrote to a friend in this country, she spoke of America as "a land in which she would never cease to take an interest."[1]

Of the spirit with which, throughout her editorial writings, Mrs. Coleridge advocated her father's character—as a man, an author, and a philosopher—it is enough to say that it was a daughter's love and a woman's strong sense of truth blended together—filial piety and earnest truthfulness in perfect harmony. On this subject it will be far better to cite her own words—both prose and—what she could at need command—a strain of exquisite moral verse.

I have not striven (she said) to conceal any of my natural partialities, or to separate my love of my father from my moral and intellectual sympathy with his mode of thought. I have endeavored to give the genuine impressions of my mind respecting him, believing that if reporters will but be honest, and study to say that and that alone which they really think and feel, the color which their opinions and feelings may cast upon the subject they have to treat of, will not finally obscure the truth. Of this I am sure, that no one ever studied my father's writings earnestly, and so as to imbibe the author's spirit, who did not learn to care still more for truth than for him, whatever interest in him such a study may have inspired.

These few lines are an attempt to bring out a sentiment, which my father once expressed to me on the common saying that "Love is blind."

> Passion is blind, not Love: *her* wond'rous might
> Informs with threefold power man's inward sight;—
> To her deep glance the soul at large displayed
> Shows all its mingled mass of light and shade:—
> Men call her blind when she but turns her head,
> Nor scans the fault for which her tears are shed.

[1]*Cf.* Letter 6, p. 77, *infra*.

Can dull Indifference or Hate's troubled gaze
See through the secret heart's mysterious maze?
Can Scorn and Envy pierce that "dread abode,"
Where true faults rest beneath the eye of God?
Not their's, 'mid inward darkness, to discern
The spiritual splendors how they shine and burn.
All bright endowments of a noble mind
They, who with joy behold them, soonest find;
And better none its stains of fraility know,
Than they who fain would see it white as snow.
—*Biog. Lit.* (ed. of 1847) p. clxxxiv.

Thus finely versified and vivified with imagination is set forth a moral truth—precious in the study alike of character and of literature.

Mrs. Coleridge took a cordial delight in correspondence with those who enjoyed her friendship; and should her letters be collected for publication, her genius and learning, and the strength and gentleness of her nature, will be seen in a very pleasing form. It is no exaggeration to say that the literature of familiar letter-writing has produced nothing which can compare with them. It is not only that they are highly intellectual and even learned compositions, but they are genuine letters withal—genuine specimens of what a woman excels in. Her letters are remarkable, indeed, for activity and reach of thought, and for varied and extensive reading; but with such gracefulness and natural ease did Mrs. Coleridge wear her endowments and her attainments, that the simple vivacity and sprightliness of the most agreeable form of familiar letter is not lost or overlaid with learning; her letters are like the animated conversation of a thoughtful and very accomplished woman—vigorous, gentle, and unpretending.[1]

[1]To enable the reader to appreciate this harmony of extraordinary female scholarship with entire simplicity and gracefulness of womanly character, he is referred to the "Appendix on the Poetical Picturesque," which Mrs. Coleridge placed at the end of her edition of the "Biographia Literaria." It is an essay of about fifteen pages in support of a critical remark of Coleridge's on "The Fairy Queen," from which Mr. Hallam and Mr. Leigh Hunt had expressed dissent. The subject is one which admitted and indeed required illustration, widely gathered from the ancient and modern poets and their commentators. Within this short essay, Mrs. Coleridge cites the poetry of the Bible, Pindar, Aeschylus, Euripides (with the commentators on the Greek drama, Hermann, Klausen, Scholefield, Sewell), Virgil, Horace, Catullus, Dante, Spenser,

Mrs. Coleridge's health had been delicate for several years, and during the last two years she was the victim of one of the most fearful maladies that flesh is heir to. Towards the end her sufferings were great, but they were borne with the utmost fortitude, her mind retaining its clearness to the last. Within only a few days of her death, she made her last effort upon an edition of her father's poems—the volume which has since been published as "edited by Sara and Derwent Coleridge." In the editorial part of that book will be found the last production of her pen—*tanquam cycnea vox et oratio*. Her filial piety never failed. No sick-room selfishness narrowed her large and generous sympathies. In her last letter to a friend in America, she said: "Of course, all literary exertion and extensive corespondence are out of the question for me in my present condition. . . . I wish to accompany [in thought] my friends in their ramblings on the face of nature, and I like to hear their views on religion, politics, morals—all subjects of general interest."[1] Speaking of her malady, she said: "I endeavour not to speculate—to make the most of each day as it comes, making use of what powers remain to me, and feeling assured that strength will be supplied, if it be sought from above, to bear every trial which my Father in Heaven may think fit to send."

This was one utterance of the Christian piety which, not only at the approach of death, but through life, was joined with the genius and learning of the daughter of Coleridge.

Philadelphia, July, 1852.

Shakespeare, Beaumont and Fletcher, Milton, Wordsworth, Coleridge, Southey, Keats, and Sir Walter Scott—Lessing, Klopstock, and Wieland. Now, when these authorities—from literature, ancient and modern, continental and English—are presented thus in succint array, and without the context, it might be thought that they could hardly have been cited, especially by a woman, without something like pedantic ostentation. But the reader, most inclined to a censorious dread of female learning, will be able to detect nothing of the kind. Everything like pedantry or display seems to be charmed away by the mere power of simple-heartedness; and one ceases to think of the extent and variety of the learning that subserves the well-reasoning earnestness with which the subject is discussed. The reader cannot but feel that it comes from the abundance of genuine scholarship, and he will, I am quite sure, be disposed to think of the writer as Charles Lamb did when he described her as "the inobtrusive, quiet soul, who has digged her noiseless way" through so much learning. [H. Reed's note.]

[1]*Cf.* Letter 6, pp. 76–7, *infra*.

II

LETTERS FROM SARA COLERIDGE TO HENRY REED

(1849–1851)

II

LETTERS FROM SARA COLERIDGE TO HENRY REED

1

My dear Sir,

I will not wait till I can have a conference with my brother, who is, as you are aware, extremely engrossed with the affairs of St Mark's College, to answer your kind letter and assure you of my cordial concurrence in your scheme[1] and approbation of it—as far as I am justified, from long attention to my Father's books and all that concerns them, in using *that* word. I am sure that my brother Derwent will think and feel generally as I do on the subject of your communications. I hope, however, to have an opportunity of talking with him soon, and if he suggested anything different or farther than what I can now say, either he himself or I will write another letter conveying his thoughts more particularly.

I am daily expecting to receive from Mr. Pickering, our Publisher, the "Notes on Shakespeare and other Dramatists, with some additions &c." This is in the main a reprint of volumes I. & II. of the "Literary Remains," but to the dramatic criticisms therein contained I have added some other critical or literary matter from manuscript *marginalia*, and a few pieces that appeared many years ago in Blackwood's Magazine. I inclose a proof of the Advertisement. From the Table Talk *we* could take nothing, except a small extract or two for

[1]On April 2, 1849, in a letter to Wordsworth Henry Reed made the following request: "Permit me to trespass on your kindness in asking you to do me the favor to forward the enclosed letter to Mrs. H. N. Coleridge. I am not quite certain as to her address, and being a stranger to her I wish also so far to avail myself of your kindness as to communicate a letter to her through you. You will, I am sure, readily do me this service, when I mention that my object in writing to Mrs. Coleridge is to endeavour to make an arrangement to secure for her an interest in the reprint of some of her Father's works in this country." This request was the beginning of the correspondence between Reed and Mrs. Coleridge.

a note, such as might fairly be considered within the limits of allowable quotation:—because that book is not our property, but was sold to Mr. Murray from the first. *You* can of course avail yourself of its contents; and now this subject is before me, I will not leave it without a few words of explanation respecting the anecdote of my father's interview with Keats, (at Vol. II. p 89—of the first edition—I have no other at hand.)

My father's companion, in his walk, to whom his remark on the *deathy feel* of Keats' hand was addressed, was his friend Mr Joseph Henry Green. Keats asked Mr. Green, with whose father-in-law he had been apprentice at Southgate, to introduce him to Mr. Coleridge, and the request was readily complied with. Mr. Green himself talked of the matter with me last September, & told me how distinctly he remembered my Father's remark on Keats' hand, which he said, "felt to Coleridge clammy and cold, like the hand of a dead man." They described the meeting &c to Mr. Gillman on their return to the Grove.

I mention these facts to you, though anecdotes do not fall within the scope of your undertaking, relying on the general interest which you appear to take in all that conerns my Father, which was worthy to be reported, because Mr. Monckton Milnes, in his *Life and Letters of Keats*, has given an utterly wrong turn to this little story. It is curious to see how *much mistake* can be crammed into a little footnote a few lines long. (This occurs in the second vol toward the end of the Memoir.) He not only metamorphoses Mr Green into Mr Leigh Hunt, with whom my Father had no personal acquaintance,—with whose opinions on politics his were most unaccordant (—spite of which, I regret, from what I have seen latterly of Mr L. Hunt's mind & disposition to judge from what he prints, that they did not know one another personally, rather than only as combatants on opposite sides of the political battlefield)—but he alters the *time* of the meeting by a difference of several years. "This was at the period," he says, "when Keats first knew Mr Hunt." Now Keats knew Mr Hunt as early as 1816. Mr Green never saw S. T. C. till 1817, & the meeting was some years afterwards—most probably in 1819, when, as Leigh Hunt says, the poet had his fatal malady upon him and knew it, tho' as my Father observed, it was not generally known—certainly was unknown to himself.

Mr Lockhart tells me that there are several other mistakes in Mr Milnes' book beside that which I have noticed. It seemed to me, in the part which proceeds from Mr Milnes himself (the publication is highly interesting in what it contains of Keats,—though the *letters* upon the whole are painful) not very judicious. Keats' fragment "The Eve of St Mark," published by Mr Milnes, is very exquisite.[1] There reigns throughout a strong desire to exalt Lord Jeffray [*sic*], not merely as a man or an author at large—but as the Editor of the Ed. Review of 30 years ago—of that Journal, which endeavoured to blot out the rising sun of poetry from the sky, to stifle it on the horizon & even when it had risen almost to meridian height, with fogs of unprincipled adverse criticism, and storm clouds of political animosity in the form of literary disapprobation and contempt. He might as well have tried to give Zoilus the name of a genial & judicious critic, as to make the poetical world now believe that the reviler of the Muse of Wordsworth, was a generous and discerning judge of the poetry of the 19th century. As for Keats—Lord J's patronage of whom is adduced as in part the ground of those lofty attributions—the Ed. Review never took him up till he was the idol of a poetical circle, and the abused and almost victimized of the Quarterly & Blackwood. The praise given him was essentially inconsistent with former censure of his predecessors, generally—as to principle—and in particulars by no means correct, as more accurate critics well acquainted with ancient classic poetry have pointed out.

But this is a digression—Had I foreseen how long it would

[1]This sentence is written in the margin of the letter with no indication of its place in the context.

stretch out—I should scarce have ventured upon it. Before I began upon the Table Talk I had it in my mind to say, that I am rejoiced at what you tell me of "valuable unpublished matter—transcripts of notes by my Father in books of Charles Lamb." I hope it will prove that they *are* new—and have never before been in print. As you possess the Literary Remains, you must be able to know the certainty of this matter. My Father's writings are so miscellaneous, and in so many different fragments, that I do not always find it easy to speak myself as to points concerning them at once without a good deal of searching and consideration. *Some* notes in books of C.L. have, I know, been published.

What you so kindly say respecting the profits of your proposed publication—I have found it more difficult to answer at once than the rest of your letter. I cannot without some hesitation express *approval* of what is so wholly calculated for our benefit—in a pecuniary point of view. And, as my Father's descendants must in any case, *as such*, have a peculiar share in the honour and credit which may redound from any thoughts of his that are given to the world, we should be under obligations to you for *profit*, on that score, so far as your work proves successful, & for your intention at all events, quite sufficient to repay us for what encouragement you may receive from our glad consent to your scheme and sincere wish that you may secure the gratitude of many readers for the accomplishment of it. I can only add my hope, in which I am sure my brother will join, that you will not consider yourself bound by what you have said, to the arrangement you propose, but will act as seems convenient on a further view of the matter, feeling assured that we shall take an interest in the book, & be well satisfied with the publication, whatever passes between you and the publisher, on the point you mention.

I speak as a daughter—I never try to speak otherwise, thinking it more *honest*—more for the promotion of truth—to shew the real thoughts of my heart undisguisedly than to affect to speak of my Father's writings as an uninterested critic. But speaking as I best may, I cannot help saying—that whatever my Father has said, that is really sound & unimportant [*sic*], is so *well* said, that I believe it will not be superseded in point of expression, but will long appear in the world of thought in the dress which he has supplied. Believe me, my dear Sir, Yours very sincerely and respectfully.

SARA COLERIDGE. April 21, *1849*.

2

Tettenhall Wood—Seat of Miss Hinckes
Staffordshire
July 3 rd *1850*.

My dear Sir,

How many months ago did I think to write to you ere many days were gone, to thank you for the address you kindly sent me by Mr Yarnall!—and to ask how I might send you a copy of the collection of my Father's newspaper writings, which I was editing! Now here we are in the very heart of summer[,] nay entered on the downward path which leads us "to the hollows, where the frosts of winter lie"—and the "Essay on his own Times by S. T. Coleridge"—so the new book is entitled for a reason which you will see stated in the Preface—has been out for some months, and my letter has been all this time postponed. I must defer it no longer, although it is not easy, in a friend's country house, full of guests coming in successive parties, whom we have been invited to meet, to find time for any but brief letters—because if my leisure is short & liable to interruption here, at home for some months or longer, it will be none at all. The various calls of a London life to a widow with children, and a Father's multifarious literary productions to take care of, are such that they render it generally out of my power to transfer from the tablet of the brain to the sheet of paper the many epistles mentally written in sleepless nights to creditor-correspondents of long standing.

I think I have not written to you in any other way than the above mentioned since I saw your friend Mr. Yarnall. Will you give my kind remembrances to him when you communicate with him & say that I look back to our last conversation with much interest, and that both my brother and I should feel much pleasure in seeing him again if he ever re-visited England. He was here at a fearful time, when the mysterious visitations of the cholera and its sudden destruction of human life kept one in a perpetual tremor. I thought with concern that he was about to go back into the cholera atmosphere of highest intensity; but he appeared calm and strong in spirit, and in the midst of pity for him I felt envy, after a sort, of his firmness and tranquillity. We have nothing of the complaint in England thus far; and the season both in this respect and as far as regards the fruits of the earth, cold & wet as it has been upon the whole, appears very favorable.

I am here with my son and daughter in a delightful country residence with our friends Miss Hinckes the mistress of this fair domain, and Mr & Mrs. Moore, her Pastor and his wife, who are as much at home in her house as she is herself. Ever since she lost her brother & parents the three have formed one family—and this union of sympathy and friendship, with no tie of blood or of law to keep it up, is as pleasing & interesting to witness as it is singular. During a great part of the year the maiden lady resides with her friends at the comparatively humble Vicarage of Eccleshall, of which wide & populous parish Mr. Moore is the active zealous parish priest:when the party are here he serves his church & attends to his smaller parish of Pen, and the Curate of Pen goes to take care of Eccleshall. The home at Tettenhall Wood is constructed and furnished all in the older style with lofty ornate hall and painted glass and carved oak balusters and moveable furniture, with remarkable elegance & great harmony of effect. The grounds are beautifully laid out in the way of landscape garden or nature improved—shaven and combed and drest,—which is quite a different thing from art making use of nature as mere material: to express myself more straight forwardly, the place here though smooth and ornate in the highest degree which the latest gardening skill can produce, is so disposed as to follow the varied lines and forms, the indefiniteness and infinitude of nature; it is most artfully managed yet the character is not artificial, like that of the older English Gardens, which are still used in France. Miss Hinckes has built and endowed a church and founded a school at Wolverhampton. I was saying yesterday to a Mr. Whately, brother of the Abp of Dublin, who has been staying here with his wife, a sister of our Lord Chancellor Lord Cottenham, and single daughter, that she has shewn the same sort of wisdom that Queen Elizabeth shewed in the choice of her ministers. Twenty years ago the house of her fathers stood here, a common-place inconvenient mansion in an ordinary garden—All the present beauty of the house & gardens of Tettenhall Wood may be called Mr Moore's creation: and his management of her affairs has enabled her to do good works, which lead people to suppose that her fortune is far larger than it really is. Yesterday we visited Pen & admired the beautiful stained glass windows which have been lately put into the Church. They look like frames of beryl stuck about with rubies [,] topazes and sapphires. Pen looks out upon the Malvern Hills of Worcestershire.

Since we have been here there has been a succession of parties of guests [,] many of the neighboring clergy [,] gentles & nobles [,] staying in the house & I wanted only more nervous strength to have had great enjoyment. As it is, there will be much of a most pleasant kind for my memory to carry away from this visit. Among the guests were Mr Herrick & his sister of Beau Manor Park in Leicestershire [,] descendants of Herrick the Poet or of his ancestors, very amiable and agreeable persons. We have had several discussions of Ruskin's theory of the superiority of the modern landscape painters over the Cuyps, Poussins and Claudes of old time. Wrong as I believe that theory to be on the whole, and as to its conclusions, both from my own observation and from the remarks of artists and pictorial critics unprofessional, with whom I have talked on the subject, I do not wonder at all to find you and other correspondents of mine in America warmly admiring and believing in his book at a distance as you are from those works of genius which he disparages. It is a book of great eloquence, though the style has the modern fault of diffuseness, and the description[s] of nature with reference to art, which it contains, are full of beauty & vivacity, evincing great powers of observation and a mind of great animation; and no doubt there is some portion of truth in what he throws out concerning the defects of the old landscape paintings. But I have no doubt that his thoughts on the whole subject when he first dashed them forth to the public were exceedingly crude, and that he was far from having perceived clearly and fully either the nature of the art of painting, or the true relations between the state of that art as exhibited in the old landscape paintings, and as it appears in our modern English school. As that accomplished artist Richmond, a great friend of Ruskin, observes, he ought, by the same principles upon which he condemns the old landscape pieces, to condemn the historical and sacred paintings of the same or an earlier age, and to these he attributes the same merits that the world has agreed to think they possess. I have heard that grand solemn picture,—the Raising of Lazarus, by Seb. del Piombo, designed by Michael Angelo,—declared unnatural and an inferior production to what modern art could produce, by an accomplished artist, who applied to it the same tests of pictorial excellence as those with which R detects the vast inferiority of Claude to Turner. Now that picture (it is in our National Gallery in London) is pronounced the most sublime composition of its kind in the world by the first connoisseurs in Europe; and yet its merits are appreciated by persons of taste and sensibility in general, even those who have no particular, or what may be called *technical*, knowledge of painting.

Then Ruskin laughs at the notion of *generalizing*—but he says nothing that shakes my faith, in the slightest degree, in the common creed of critics on this point. Milton generalizes in word-painting in the fourth-book of "Paradise Lost"; his description of the Garden of Eden brings together all the lovely appearances of nature which are to be found in all beautiful countries of the warm & temperate zones, not a single object which is peculiar to any one place in particular. His Eden is an abstract, a quintessence of the beautiful features of our Mother Earth's fair face, and who shall say, or what man of sense and sensibility has ever yet said, that this *generalized* picture was painted on a wrong principle? Now what Miton has done in words, Claude, to my thinking, has done with the pencil; and all Turner's finest and most famous pictures are offsprings of Claude's genius. Turner was called "the English Claude" when he was at the height of his fame, and his beautiful Dido & Eneas or Rise of Carthage never would have been painted as it is painted but for these splendid prototypes, as I think they may be called, from the hand of Claude, in which sea, sky and city are combined after a manner of his own, which I scruple not to say *reports* of the combiner's mind as much as of the material furnished by the world without. What Ruskin *meant* I undertake not to say. I very much doubt his having any certain definite consistent meaning made out in his own mind when he undertook to reform the opinions of mankind on the subject of painting, on the point I am about to mention; but he *says*, what I believe to be as great a mistake as can be entertained on this particular point, that a painter has nothing to do but produce as close a copy as possible of particular objects and combinations of objects in nature. The fact is, that the works of every great painter are recognized as the products of an individual mind; if it was not for this individual *subjective* character I believe they would be utterly uninteresting. May we not arrive at the truth of the matter by ascertaining what is and ought to be the painter's aim when he employs himself in imitating the natural landscape on canvas: surely it is not to make the spectator acquainted with some particular spot or set of objects; it is to produce a work of *art*, not to present a camera lucida copy of nature; it is not merely to call up the identical feelings which the very contemplation of the natural landscape itself is apt to excite, but to *remind* us of those feelings in conjunction with the sense of the presence of an individual mind and character, pervading and presiding over the whole. We may not, in looking at a Cuyp or a Hobbima, a Claude or a Salvator Rosa, *explain to ourselves* the source of our interest in the picture and its peculiar character; and yet it may be the impress of an individual genius, of this man's or that man's frame of intellect and inspiration, that delights us when we contemplate a fine landscape painting far more than anything else. The old painters were superior to the moderns, in my opinion, because an individual mind was stamped upon their works more powerfully and impressively; their paintings have more *character;* it is *that* which I look for in these works of *art*. I do not go to them to improve my knowledge of nature.

This is a difficult subject and I am aware that I have been expressing myself broadly and laxly & and perhaps have gone as far from the exact truth on one side as Ruskin on the other. But this I do deliberately think or at least strongly suspect, that as the power of representing nature on canvas must necessarily be very limited, and is rather suggestion than presentation, the attempt to imitate the outward object beyond a certain point may injure the general effect of the work as a whole, and that those departures from truth which Ruskin points out in the old masters as faults and deficiencies may be a part of their power and merit of their works as suggestive compositions. I believe that they did quite right to address themselves to the common eye of mankind, not to the eye of the painter; they present clouds and woods as we see them when we rather feel their loveliness than think about it, or examine into it. Turner has aimed at cramming into a piece of canvas or paper a foot square or less as much as possible of all that he sees in an actual sky on a certain day of the year, and has succeeded so well, that critics complain of his skies as "top-heavy." I have heard a clever engraver say that some of them owt [*sic*] to be turned upside down; that they are solid enough to stand upon. It is impossible, in the too eager devotion to *truth*, to *all* the truth of the sky and her appurtenances, to do justice to earth and exhibit the due relations of solidity between her and the firmament above her.

A very accomplished and intelligent artist of my acquaintance [,] Samuel Laurence—a portrait painter in oils and in chalks[,] had a long discussion with Ruskin on the subject of his book, I did not myself hear that discussion, but his impression was that the author quite failed in defending it, and this I can believe, because he has virtually retracted some of its most important positions, and I have never yet met any great admirer and student of pictures, who was an entire convert to his doctrine. He declared to a friend of mine that he wished to be understood, in his high attributions to Turner, to be referring only to his *water-colour* productions. But certainly this is not reconcilable with the language of his book. I have ever been a very warm admirer, and ardent defender of Turner against his ordinary assailants. He is a poetical painter, and gives me more delight than any other modern artist. But Ruskin is extravagant and defends him in part I think on wrong grounds. If Ruskin is right no one can appreciate Turner but Turner himself. No doubt every great creator must teach the world how & what to admire; but if he does not succeed in being admired in the end he has not done the work he pretends to do. No doubt Ruskin says rightly, that a painter must aim at *truth* in his representations, but the question is *how much* truth he can obtain without sacrificing the general effect,—the emotions which the *whole* is to produce; and I think he goes upon a wrong, because one-sided, principle, when he argues as if the only merit of a painting is its truthful representation of the outward object, a certain *mode* of doing this derived from the painter's individual mind in that which interests beholders more than aught beside, and I think I am referring to *fact*, when I say it is *this* principally which assigns *value* to the picture. The pictures of Claude are not so *true* as those of many a painter whose works are now not worth anything in the market—Glover's for instance, which people bought eagerly on their first appearance, because they were so *like* the places of which they were portraits. Ruskin is quite mistaken too, I think, in his remarks on the distinction made by my Father and others between the terms "imitation and copying." Aristotle in the Art of Poetry a standard authority has used the former in the broad general sense, which Ruskin seems to suppose *not* the proper one, to produce a likeness of some object of observation, by art, the intention of which is not that it should pass for the original, by way of delusion, but to delight the spectator by the very sense of the art exercised. "Othello" is an imitation of a domestic story in which the passion of jealousy was the principal feature and the chief mover of the event. Now Burke says, quite in accordance with this usual meaning of the terms, "whenever we are delighted by the representation of things which we should *not* delight to see in reality, the pleasure arises from *imitation*." I have not Ruskin's book at hand. But I remember he says upon this—"the very contrary is the case"—because, in his hastiness of judgment, he determines that *imitation* properly means no more than *copying* —the mere production of a duplicate or facsimile of the original. Usage decides the meaning of terms, & I think it is against him. Even etymology, as far as it goes, is against him; for *imitation* comes from the Greek word, which we render by "*mimicry*"; and he who mimics another never means to pass for the man he mimics by disguise; the pleasure he gives rests upon the spectator's sense that the likeness is presented in a medium of diversity.

It is time to conclude this rambling epistle. Before you receive it you will have heard of the sad event which puts our papers in mourning, the death of Sir R. Peel by a fall from his horse. I am one of those who honour Peel as a practical statesman: I am no politician, and always speak on such subjects, with reserve on account of my inadequate insight. But we cannot help seeing or seeming to see some broad facts and acts in connection with them. It seems to me that Peel had the sagacity to see when the time had arrived what this country required, and *would have*, either from him or some one else, with more or less of struggle and commotion and that he had the resolution to do what he had come to think under the circumstances necessary, let men say what they might, let him lose office or retain it. If he acted upon self-interest—it was not of the vulgar kind, but of that which was one with the good of the country; he would preserve the character of a statesman, who would not sacrifice the public advantage to his own reputation for consistency. To say, he should have let others do what he would not do himself, with all the chances of their omitting to do it—or deferring to do it, seems to me a *wordy*, superficial, unpractical way of putting the matter.

You will see by the public prints, how the Gorham controversy has been stirring up the Church. It seems to some few of my High Church friends that the judgment of the Judicial committee was right, both as regards truth and expediency: that it did but assert a *fact*, which cannot be disproved; that the Church of England inclines to the view of universal infant regeneration—regeneration being understood as an *inward* change—but has not, either in practice or formally, the whole matter being considered, so decided the question that it can be justifiable to exclude from the temporalities of the Church those who hold with Hooker that only the *elect*—in the sense of the finally saved—are really regenerated. As my friend here—certainly a strong Churchman and Tory—observes—our Church plainly admits the doctrine of Predestination in the Calvinistic sense. She must therefore allow all the direct consequences of the doctrine. The struggle has shewn however that the popular High Church party are stronger & more numerous in proportion to Evangelicals and Churchmen, like my Father, of the more philosophical sort, than I thought they were. Thousands have protested against the judgment who have ever been opposed to Tractarianism & semi-Romanism—because they do not perceive, what seems to me, clearly proveable, that this dogma of momentary regeneration can be maintained only on essentially Romish principles. The men who maintain it now scientifically and as part of a system, teach a very different doctrine of regeneration *upon the whole* from that of our old divines, whose opinions upon infant baptism, they took into catenas to persuade passive readers that their view is only old Anglicanism revived. Our old divines teach that regeneration is a change of the whole man—a change of *mind:* such a change cannot be contained within a ritual moment; consequently *infant* regeneration, in their representation, is essentially distinct from the new birth of *an adult.* It is but the first stage in the entire process of the great change of the flesh into the spirit, and in stating what this *incipiency,* this first step is in essence, they are not very intelligible or consistent. Sometimes they represent it as a mere relative sanctification—the reception of a claim or title to the blessings of the covenant; sometimes they call it an inward presence of the Holy Spirit—a "creation of life" in the infant soul; & how this can be maintained if Regeneration is what the Apostles all describe it, a change of mind & character, by *faith, through knowledge of the truth,*—John I 12. 1 Peter I 22, 23. James I 18 [.1]John V 1.2 Cor III 17, 18. Rom VIII 14–29 &c &c &c especially if it be ascribed to *all* infants alike, those who prove good & those who prove evil, I cannot imagine. Burnet & Waterland state the office of Baptism, in my opinion, rightly as giving a claim to the blessings of the Covenant, but without immediate unconditional effects. But Waterland denied the term regeneration to the moral & spiritual change and appropriated it to Baptism—because Baptism had been called Regeneration by the Early Christians, as it had been indeed—by Jews and Pagans before the coming of our Lord. Now this may be but change of a *name*; but names cannot be wrongly applied without causing confusion of mind and error in regard to *things*. I believe that if Waterland had taken a more clear consistent manly course in the matter our present dissensions would have been precluded or at least greatly weakened. What a perverted state of thought is indicated in the assertion, that the Regeneration of the human soul is *not* the most radical and general change which the human being can undergo—that it is *not* renovation—or that to be regenerate is *not* the same thing as to be "a new creature in Christ!"

With many apologies for this hurried letter I remain dear Sir,
Yours with much respect

SARA COLERIDGE

I should be much interested to hear any account of your pursuits and literary undertakings or aught else that occupies your attention of general concern when you have leisure to write.

I fear this letter will seem both dull and incorrect. It has been written interruptedly and I have slipped into descriptions of the people and places around me, forgetting how impossible it is to convey by a few sentences or perhaps by any number of words a notion worth having of such distant objects.

3

[Apparently enclosed with the preceding letter]

10 Chester Place
Regents Park
July 22nd 1850

My dear Sir,

I was unable to despatch my letter to you from Staffordshire because uncertain of your address. I now find that your last is dated from Philadelphia and hope that direction will be sufficient. After writing to you I saw a great deal of the beauty of Staffordshire—which is indeed a lovely sylvan country, full of beautiful residences of nobles and gentles and pretty elegant clerical abodes. I saw Trentham—the princely residence of the Duke of Sutherland, and admired the grand scale and elegant style of all the ministrative useful part of the establishment, so exclusively—as far as Europe is concerned, the English nobleman's appurtenances. The pleasure ground is of more questionable taste. To me the ten acres of flower garden appeared somewhat unmeaning—too like a vast nursery for flowers & shrubs [.] Some compare it to fairy-land, but it is too artificial for that—it lacks some principal charms of nature, clear streams & crystal lakes and foamy rainbowy waterfalls with nooks in which the pure element is transmuted, by some strange optical alchemy, from crystal to beryl & from beryl to emerald. There are waters at Trentham; but alas! they are not clear & this want of water is Staffordshire's great defect. The house is full of elegance and abounds in paintings, but has no one grand room—no really fine picture—only some beautiful statues. The *house*, however, ought not to be criticised, because it was *intended* to be simple and merely comfortable—the town residence was to have all the fine pictures & to be the shew place—& Dunrobin, the mansion now in progress in Sutherland, will I suppose be a model of all that is stately and superb in a ducal residence.

Before my return I staid at Beau Manor Park the residence of Mr Herrick, a descendant of Sir William Herrick—an ambassador to Queen Elizabeth. Herrick the poet is among his ancestors & has a place in the gorgeous [?] painted window, emblazoned with all the Herrick heraldry, which admits light into the very grand & imposing hall. This abode is, as far as my knowledge goes, the acme of modern magnificent comfort. The sleeping rooms are all furnished in the style of elegant London drawing rooms with rich silk hangings, brilliant Brussells carpets & rugs, ebony or carved oak furniture, mirrors in splendid gilt frames [,] the most exquisite vessels of Derbyshire ware &c &c The very extensive Park is full of the noblest oaks I ever saw—The oak is the weed of that Leicestershire district as the elm is in England generally; & Mr H. when he came to his estate had only to clear judiciously. The owner of all this accumulation of luxury & splendour—one of the richest commoners in England—is one of the most amiable men in it—his heart as faithful [,] kind & affectionate as his manners are frank [,] simple and cordial. He and his kindly courteous sister, who presides over his establishment, seem *made for society*—and indeed, as they are generally entertaining about 20 people, practice would tend to make them perfect, in addition to their natural fitness & capabilities. Mr Herrick is an excellent specimen of the wealthy English gentleman of old family—and the broad oaks of his Park seem quite appropriate to him & representative of his nature.

[Unsigned]

4

10 Chester Place
November 29th 1850

My dear Friend

Many thanks to you for two most interesting volumes. The "Descriptive Sketches" with your *inscription*, is a very gratifying present to me. I have always wished to possess early editions of Mr Wordsworth's works, but have not been able to lay hold of many. I cannot bear the arrangement of his poems in the later editions by subject, without regard to date. The *tone* of the productions of the Poets second & third æras is as unlike that of his great vigorous day, as a picture of Stanfield to one by Claude or Poussin—& who would mix modern paintings in a gallery, with those of the old hands? I remember seeing an exhibition of Cal[l]cott's landscape paintings in the third room of the British Gallery, ancient masters occupying the first and second. You can hardly imagine the deadening effect upon them. They were reduced to *chalk* and water. Any believer in Ruskin, I think, must have been staggered by that most odious or at least injurious comparison and contrast. Not that I do not admire Ruskin's *first* book. It has *great merits*, but it never converted or *per*verted me from Claude & Cuyp & S Rosa, though it made me more than ever, if *possible*, a worshipper of the great Mistress of all painters—Nature.

The edition of Gray & your Memoir are a valuable addition to my library. I possess the Eton Edition & had lately been reading Mitford's Memoir, which rendered yours all the more interesting. Your's ought to supersede every other.

I think your conclusion about Gray's poetic powers, is the truth of the matter. The author of the Elegy, *admirable* as his poetry is, *in its line*, could never, I think, under any circumstances, have helped to found a new school of poetry. His mind did not present a broad enough surface for the spirit of the Age to operate on, even if the new age, which moulded & was moulded by, the last generation of poets & romancers, had set in while he was in his vigour. No new aspect of humanity or of nature is exhibited in his writings. Even Cowper was, in my opinion, far more original as to thought and way of viewing things. And the personal character of Cowper was more broad, bold & interesting than that of Gray[.]

I am reperusing with great delight the *Scotch* novels of Walter Scott. I do not think "Ivanhoe" and the later works not on Scottish ground, at all to be reckoned among the great influencive literary productions of the age—productions of genius, along with "Waverley," "Guy Mannering," "The Antiquary" (perhaps the best of all), "Rob Roy," "The Black Dwarf" (which has been underrated) [,] "Old Mortality," "The Heart of Mid Lothian" & "The Bride of Lammer Muir." [*sic.*]

"The Black Dwarf" has an especial merit in exhibiting the odd *mixture* of feeling and opinions on particular subjects which may exist in uneducated, unreflective minds. Hobbie is persuaded that Father Elshie has dealings with the Evil One, and would try to prejudice his salvation if he had an opportunity—yet is willing to receive a benefit at his hands, and is grateful for it and is affectionately disposed toward the donor as if he believed him as "*canny*" as other folks. The tale however was overshadowed by the superior merit of "Old Mortality" and no doubt it has more than the ordinary amount of absurdity in the foundation.

To complete my account of Mr de Vere author of the critique at p 173– he is a very dear friend & connection of the author of "Philip Von Artevelde," who married his first cousin, the youngest daughter of Lord Monteagle (Spring Rice.) His father, whose sonnets are interesting Wordsworthianisms, was a nephew of the late Earl of Limerick. He—the Earl of L. I fear, was but an indifferent Irish Landlord—Lord Monteagle, who married his daughter—since his second marriage with Miss Marshall—eldest daughter of the great Leeds Manufacturer & a very superior woman—of high principles & a strong sense of Christian duty—has been a very disinterested and right-acting one. O si sic omnes!

Mr de Vere has been writing a great deal on Emigration and Colonization—the only resource for Ireland. His Edinboro article on that subject is admirable.

The North British Review begins to be much admired here. I should like to know who wrote the article on Wordsworth, which I am going to read. I hear it much praised.

That is a beautiful poem by John Moultrie, prefixed to Gray's poems. I wish I could send you a copy of his "Black Fence"—an anti-Papal-aggression poetical effusion. On my telling him that I thought F. Newman and his Straussism infinitely more formidable than J H Newman and his Romanism with Wiseman, Ullathorne, the Pope himself & his whole College to help it forward he replies "I fear Frank more than John Newman & his compeers—but as a parish priest my battle is with Romanism—& in coy Romanism I am strongly beleaguered.—I have in my parish one of Pugins Romish Chapels, a monastery with 8 or 9 monks—the sister of Henry Martin's biographer as a sister of charity—an R. C. College about to open with Henry Wilberforce (brother of our Bishop of Oxford) as its chief Professor—and for one of my nearest neighbors a Romish proselyte—of immense wealth and spite of his 'Old English Gentleman' type, as thoroughly priest- and confessor-ridden as you think it impossible for one of that class ever to become."

Some who wish well to our Church, say they fear after all the violent excitements of the present hour on account of the Papal Aggression, a strong reaction. But I own I rejoice in the demonstration. The fear and anger of this crisis will of course subside—but what has taken place proves and will shew the Romanists & Romanizers, that there is a deep seated wide spread aversion to Popery in this fair realm of England, which will come into effective action whenever any attempt is made to re-introduce a form of religion which is the natural and necessary enemy to liberty in all times and in every place.

I cannot agree with Cuthbert Southey, who thinks that we are straining at a gnat after swallowing the camel of Emancipation. There was nothing that insulted and endangered our Church in a Romanist's sitting in Parliament directly—and the principles of toleration & equal dealing with all religions, *as such*, seemed to demand the concession. But this act, is in reality, a political movement—and ought to be politically resisted. My Uncle Southey could have refused Emancipation in the *foresight* of this & similar aggressions—but it was better to give them *rope* enough to strangle their own cause in the hearts of the whole nation. Now no man can say that the intolerance & ambition of Romanism are obsolete—all must see that it is a born Ishmael—its hand is against every other form of religion and every other form must keep a controlling hand upon it.

The case in Ireland—in matter of *feeling* at least—is very different as it seems to me. *There* Popery is the national religion —& it must ever be felt as a hardship that it is excluded from the place it formerly occupied & deprived of the property it once possessed.

I have written in haste—perforce—& must beg excuse for a scrawl which is a sad contrast to your fine writing.

Believe me with many thanks and much regard your faithful friend Sara Coleridge.

Will you remember me very kindly to Mr Yarnall.

[Across the top of the first page of the letter is written:]

The book (Gray) is beautiful in paper and type. The engravings are rather black but I should think very good. What a well known scene to my eyes is that of the river at Eton, known in itself & by Evans' many pictures!

5

10 Chester Place
Regent's Park
May 19–21–*1851*

My dear Mr. Reed,

Your late communications have interested me warmly and gratified me deeply. Never since I received them have I been in such a state of easy health and leisure as are necessary for answering such letters as elaborately and as carefully as they excite in me a desire to answer them; yet I might have begun some sort of reply much earlier, but that Mr de Vere has deprived me of the power of referring to one portion of them by leaving the sheet at Curra[g]h Chase, (his brother's seat near Dublin where he usually resides.) on his last coming to England. He will dine here today to meet Mr Moore, the Vicar of Eccleshall, his wife and Miss Hinckes of Tettenhall Wood, the picturesque and in some sort poetical residence, whence I wrote to you last year (Now I bethink me it was to other foreign correspondents—yes it *was* to you—) and I shall have an opportunity of *attacking* him on his neglect. He has been carrying on a controversy with me about Archdeacon Wilberforce's scheme of Regeneration, which I cannot, in spite of many reams of paper covered with eloquence from his pen, perceive to be really reconcilable either with the truths of Revelation on the subject, which in themselves are plain enough to be understood by the meanest capacity, but which have been, as I think, purposely obscured and misrepresented by an embroidered veil of dogmatism gradually woven over them, or rather a succession of veils, supplied by different ages, laid one over the other—either with the truths of Revelation or with the laws of human thought, which the philosopher in his study views abstractly, and which the man of common sense in practical life constantly assumes in discourse and proceeds upon in conduct. Mr de Vere admits, as indeed what thoughtful person can deny, that the spirit of man is the intelligent will,—that the will is the spiritual in humanity. Does it not seem inevitably to follow from this fundamental position, that a divinely restored spiritual nature must have its seat in the will—must in truth *be*, or consist in, a holy condition of the will itself, that is a state of subjection to the Holy Spirit; for *so* alone can the human will be holy? This is the dictate of reason, and it coincides exactly with the declarations of Scripture: "they that are *led by the Spirit* of God they are the sons of God": and "Whosoever has been born of God doth not commit sin; for His seed remaineth in him, and he *cannot* sin because he hath been born of God."

No man is *absolutely* sinless; but we mean by *a good man* one who has a general character of goodness,—in whom good predominates; who acts justly and kindly and mercifully in all the great leading matters of human life, and does wrong in minor points of comparatively slight concern. Surely we may define the sons of God after the same rule, and take them to be men who are good in the main and in the general tenor of their lives, because their will is *in the main* under divine influence. The idea of a son of God or a regenerate person differs from the general notion of a good man only in this, that it refers more expressly to a moral character resulting from religious principle produced by divine grace, whereas in thinking of a *good man*, which is a wider term, we do not decide *how* he is good—whether by force of natural disposition or by knowledge of the truth and faith in God under the influence of God's Holy Spirit.

Now it seems to me that Mr de Vere departs from these plain principles and brings confusion into his thoughts by insisting upon that ancient *chimera*, as I cannot but think it, of inherited *guilt*—an evil nature which is distinct both from actual sinfulness, and from that proneness to sin and weakness of will, which is never in any degree removed or counteracted except by acts of the will itself, freely submitting to divine power,—which infuses into it strength to resist temptation and this strength is that inability to sin which alone is perfect *freedom*—the glorious liberty of the children of God.

Is not all this plain & bright, as the sun at noon day?—But the sun may be hidden by clouds, and these great sunbeamy Gospel & Reason Truths have been obscured by the miserable sacramentary system of the middle ages, which grew out of sacerdotal ambition and the sensuous materializing mode of thought imported into Christianity, in its earlier stages, from Paganism. In accordance with this system, which Mr deVere has taken up with the utmost ardour, he supposes an evil nature in the soul, distinct from the proneness of the will to evil, which certainly is not removed in baptism, to be displaced by a divine nature, which is to act *upon* the will and convert it. This supposition seems to me to involve endless contradictions. The will is the sole active power in the soul—the man himself considered as self determinant. A new nature in the soul acting upon the will is a second active principle in the one man! How is this consistent with the unity of the human spirit?

Archdeacon Wilberforce lays it down, that there is in man a principle of personality, of individuality, of responsibility, of personal ideality, which is a distinct thing from that general human nature which is the heritage of the race. Why does he make this distinction—why does he *practically* divide, where he ought only to distinguish mentally? Plainly from the vain endeavour, the eager but blind wish, to prove that one who from the earliest commencement of his course as a moral agent has been habitually resisting the Spirit of Holiness, may yet have received, and, if he be not reprobate, may still possess, as an inward gift and condition of soul, a new, divine, Christ-restored nature, not *in the will itself* & constituting the state of the will, but acting upon the will *from without*, although within the soul, and converting it or being resisted by it, as the case may be. W.'s root principle seems to me to be a false unwarrantable assumption. Our will *is—constitutes*—our general spiritual nature and personality inheres in it, as roundness in an orange or any globular object. As it would be absurd to say that the orange might be marmaladized and its rotundity "remain" unmollified by the action of the fire and the interpenetration of the power of sugar, so surely it is absurd to suppose the soul of a man regenerated by the reception of a new divine nature, while the Personality "remains" free to be regenerated or not, as it chuses: for this in plain homely language is the sense (or *non*-sense?—) of the doctrine. I must apologize for my culinary simile—I did not intend to lower—even W.'s rationale, much less the sacred subject of baptismal regeneration, by a disparaging comparison. I slipped unawares from the idea of a sphere to the lively glowing globe of the orange, a little vegetable sun—the fruit-counterpart of the sunflower—and then I had to *affect* the orange, to refine, soften, subdue, *preserve*, impregnate with a rich and grateful quality. All this made the marmalade simile almost irresistible, and after all many a pious old divine has used even a humbler in illustration of divine spiritualities. Old Latimer would not have scrupled at it. You will justly observe that the coarseness of past ages is not to be imported into the present, apart from their vigour—But I mentioned the homely comparisons of old times not to *justify* mine but to shew they are no evidence of want of earnestness or even of seriousness.

But I must break away from this subject altogether into one of a different sort—"like"—indeed—because full of reference to the moral & spiritual. "Yet oh! how different!"

The Poet Wordsworth & his Poetry differ from Theology as the speculative Intellect & Intelligence of man, from Practical Reason and the Will. I dare say that you and your friend Mr Yarnall have lately been dwelling a good deal on the two-volume Memoir of Wordsworth—which I finished slowly perusing last night in my hours of wakefulness. For, alas! I sleep but every other night,—the intervening one is now almost wholly sleepless. Mr H. C. Robinson requested that I would use the pencil or pen freely on the margins of his copy. The more notes the better. I fear he will be greatly disappointed by what I have written, and I almost wish it rubbed out, it is so trifling & in some instances not to the purpose —as I fear the owner of the book will think. I knew—and honor dear Mr Wordsworth perhaps as well as I have ever known any one in the world—more intimately than I knew my Father, and as intimately as I knew my Uncle Southey. There was much in him to know and the lines of his character were deep and strong,—the whole they formed simple and impressive. His discourse as compared with my Father's was as the Latin language to the Greek, or to borrow a comparison which has been applied to Shakespeare and Milton, as statuary to painting: it was intelligible at once and easily remembered. But in my youth when I enjoyed such ample opportunities of taking in his mind, I listened to "enjoy" and not to "understand," much less to report and inform others. In our spring time of life we are poetical, not literary, and often absorb unconsciously the intellectual airs that blow, or stilly dwell, around us, as our bodies do the fragrant atmosphere of May, full of the breath of primroses and violets, and are nourished thereby without reflecting upon the matter, any more than we classify and systematize after Linnaeus or Jussieu the vernal blossoms which delight our outward senses. I used to take long walks with Mr Wordsworth about Rydal & Grasmere and sometimes, though seldomer, at Keswick, to his Applethwaite cottage, listening to his talk all the way; and for hours have I often listened when he conversed with my Uncle, or in doors at Rydal Mount when he chatted or harangued to the inmates of his household or the neighbours. But I took no *notes* of his discourse either on the tablet of memory or on material paper: my mind and turns of thought were gradually moulded by his conversation and the influences under which I was brought by his means in matters of intellect, whilst in those which concerned the heart and the moral being I was still more, more deeply and importantly indebted to the character and daily conduct of my admirable Uncle Southey. Yet I never adopted the opinions of either *en masse*, and since I have come to years of secondary and more mature reflection I have been unable to retain many which I received from them. The impression upon my feelings of their minds remains unabated in force, but the formal views and judgments which I received from their lips, are greatly modified, though not more than they themselves modified and readjusted their own views and judgments from youth to age. I have felt deep interest in going through Dr. Wordsworth's *compilation* of fragments and scraps of the great man's life of thought and action, and think it does credit to the biographer's industry and to his discretion and good nature, though its merits as a literary performance are but negative. It does not positively misrepresent the subject, as Pickersgill's portrait, with neat shiny boots, velvet waistcoat, and sombre sentimentalism of countenance misrepresents him, but it exhibits him partially [,] disproportionately and brokenly, as one sees the oars of a boat, half in half out of the water; it puts his life-landscape also to my eye not a little out of perspective. Mr. Henry Taylor says, I think, quite justly, that the biographer has undertaken a subject of which he knows nothing, except externally & superficially, and has performed his task in a business-like way; and would have done better if he had confined himself to a business-like unpretending style throughout: the worst of his performance being the little attempts at independent poetical criticism & *purpureal patches* of high-flown moral & literary declamation which he introduces here & there. Dr Ch. Wordsworth is an able writer in his own way, and as a controversial theologian displays great vivacity—sometimes approaching to wit, and considerable information, with I suppose a sufficiency of logical dexterity; but of poetry and speculative spirituality I believe him to have very little, at first hand; his relative estimate of his great Uncle's poetical production seems to me to prove that he has but a dim and partial intuition of the Wordsworthian genius. I doubt whether he sees or feels the measureless distance between such *essential* poetry as that of Wordsworth in its true generic character, its vigorous youth & manhood, and such verse as that of Mr. Keble, which gives evidence of a refined and poetical cast of thought, but not I should say, except in a slight degree, of creative power or poetic imagination. It is only a certain proportion of the large mass of persons who read poems and like to have favourite subjects of thought adorned—or to express myself humbly—*smartened* up with conventional poetic diction, who really like poetry *per se* or thought essentially poetical, and which would evaporate in any attempt to exhibit it in prose. To these Dr W. does not seem to belong, and if so, he must be incapable of appreciating what is *immortal* in his Uncle's productions; the vital portion, by virtue of which the mass will continue to exist in the minds of men. Are you not amused by his thinking it necessary to apologize for the "Lines on revisiting the Wye &c" and buttress them up by the "Evening Voluntaries"? as if one should call upon Pugin to strengthen some of our old Cathedrals by his modern additions. Certainly if Wordsworth's Muse would be convicted of an irreligious Pantheism by that noble and exquisitely modulated poetic strain, Pantheistic she is and practically must be, whatever the *man* Wordsworth, in the late decline of his genius, thought fit to say in verse. The "Evening Voluntaries" can never piece out Lines on revisiting the Wye, "The Leechgatherer" the "Old Cumberland Beggar," "Ode on intimations of Immortality," and *id genus omne* of his poems, whatever it may tell us of Mr Wordsworths state of feeling and convictions in the latter years of his life.

You express surprise at something I let fall in a former letter on what I consider the difference and inferiority in kind of Mr W's late poems from those of his youth & middle age. I must own that I do see this very strongly, and should as little think of comparing that on the Power of Sound with the Platonic Ode, or the "Song at the Feast of Brougham Castle" as—what shall I say? the Crystal Palace with Windsor Castle or the grand carved sideboard in the former with the broad oak of the Forest, when its majestic stem of strong & solid wood is robed in foliage of tender mellow green. Those earlier odes seem to be *organic wholes*—the first of them is in some sort an image of the individual spirit of which it is an efflux. The energy & felicity of its language is so great that every passage and every line of it has been received into the poetical heart of this country, and has become the common expression of certain moods of mind & modes of thought which had hardly been developed before its appearance. The ode on the Power of Sound like "The Triad" is an elegant composition by a poetic artist—a poetical will-work, not as a whole, I should say, a piece of inspiration, though some lines in it are breathings of the poetic spirit. Mr de Vere, who has often maintained the equality if not superiority of the later Wordsworthian poems against my strong view of their decided inferiority in imaginative power, and all great poetic qualities, (*he* does not much admire "The Waggoner," & I have sometimes told him that my admiration of Wordsworth more than makes up in the intensity of degree what it wants of his in extensive quantity, & that almost all the *deepest* & most solid admirers of the Poet rest his name as a great producer chiefly on his works of the early and middle period, up to the "White Doe" inclusive)—marks for admiration in the former the last four lines of stanza 2—do of st. 3. with the last line

"A stream as if from one full heart."

The second 4 lines of st. 4 "For the tired slave" &c and "Glistens with a livelier ray" which reminds me of my Father's early lines

> "Those Hours on rapid pinions flown,
> Shall yet return, by Absence crowned,
> *And scatter livelier roses round.*"[1]

By the bye the authoress of "Emilia Wyndham," "Mount Sorel," the "Admiral's Daughter," those first notes of female genius, Mrs Marsh, has assured me warmly more than once that *she* thinks my father the greatest poet of his age, & the first mind altogether. She sees in his poetry an exquisite quality beyond that displayed in any other & making up for smallness of quantity. Some persons of literary power & keen poetic feeling beside her have expressed a similar opinion to me. A correspondent in Ceylon, Archdeacon Bailey, says he agrees perfectly with my relative estimate of S. T. C. & W W as Poets; never read any which he so agreed in—(I had assigned the superiority on the whole to the latter)—[and] thinks with me that the latter covered a larger space. I do not subscribe to some of Professor Wilson's sentences upon this subject,—as for instance the opinion implied in calling Wordsworth Coleridge's "Master." My Father had no *master* among his contemporaries in poetry. He himself was in great measure the head & founder, I believe, of the Shelley, Keats & Tennyson school in the more sensuous part of his poetry; but I think he combined more of the intellectual with this vein than his successors. It is not true in fact that W.W. was his *master* in any department of intellect except as one great mind must ever help to inform another with which it has intercourse; and my Father's poetical productions are so different in character from Wordsworth's, so far as they report of the individual, not of the age, that Wilson might as well have called Dante the master of Ariosto, or Cowper the master of Burns, or Scott or Moore of Byron, as the Author of the

[1]Lines 14–16 of *Absence: a Farewell Ode on Quitting School for Jesus College, Cambridge 1791.*

"Cumberland Beggar" and the "Excursion" the poetic Master of the Bard of "Christabel" [,] the "Ancient Mariner," and "Love" and the "Ode to Dejection."

This is a long digression from the Ode on Sound & I must go back to note, after my friend de Vere, the Theocritean passage in stanza X as far as "wild-flowers crowned," and the fine lines in st. XI at the beginning. Mr de Vere has stroked too in st. V.

> "Mounts with a tune, that travels like a blast
> Piping through cave and battlemented tower."

I see in the Memoir that Mr Wordsworth speaks of "The Triad" as containing some of the happiest verses he ever wrote. Mr Wordsworth in his great poetic day would have felt, that a few happy verses do not make a good poem. The third part of the Triad, from "Last of the three though eldest born" is extremely elegant, verse such as none but a great poetic artist could have produced. The lines in the middle division, "She stops—is fastened to that rivulet's side," to "Bland composure of eternal youth" are very fine. The lines on Lucida are a good imitation of one of the choruses in the Sampson [*sic*] Agonistes, unintended perhaps at the time of composition, but hardly I should think unrecognized by the Poet afterwards. But I confess, at the risk of lowering my taste in your esteem, which I should be right sorry to do, yet not liking to retain credit by mere suppression of a part of my mind, a serious and decided part, which has stood assaults of poetic reasoning of no small force and animation, I do confess that I have never been able to rank "The Triad" among Mr. Wordsworths immortal works of genius. It is just what he came into the poetical world to condemn, and both by practice and theory to supplant—it is, to my mind, *artificial and unreal*. There is no truth in it as a whole—although bits of truth glazed and magnified are embodied in it—as in the lines "Features to old ideal grace allied," a most unintelligible allusion to a likeness discovered in dear Dora's contour of countenance to the great

Memnon head in the British Museum, with its overflowing lips and width of mouth, which seems to be typical of the ocean. The poem always strikes me as a mongrel—an amphibious thing, neither portrait nor ideal, but an ambiguous cross between the two. Mr de Vere, before he knew me, took it for a personification of Faith [,] Hope & Charity, taken in reverse order, a sufficient proof, I think, that it is extravagant and unnatural as a description of three young ladies of the 19th century. This he will never allow, which, I tell him, is because he does not *care for truth* as I do. It is rather the habit of his mind to idealize *ad libitum*. In religious controversy he is too apt to overlook *fact*, or assume it to be such as suits his theory. This propensity his Uncle Lord Monteagle complains of his indulging in debate when he argues at length in favour of Popery. He compares the actual Church of England, as so many admirers of Romanism do, with an Ideal Church of Rome, confounding as I think superficial uniformity with vital unity, and all the pretensions of our Adversary are true because they would be so fine if they were true. Tradition and Testimony he arranges very much *ad libitum:* Primitive Christianity is infallible as reflecting the Apostolic Revelation immediately, *when it exhibits his mystical opinions*, but in all that portion of its teaching which cannot be reconciled with Literature & Mediaeval Dogmatism, it is imperfect, undeveloped—and is to be absorbed and reproduced in the mind of the Middle Ages. He does not seem to consider that the *fact* on points of this kind is generally far more matter of debate than the import & value of the fact if clearly ascertained. Few men, for instance, would venture to oppose a veritable, absolute, clearly-marked Catholic consent—the unbiassed judgment of the wisest & best informed men in every age up to the present.

But this, if a defect, is the defect, of a large & beautiful intellect. Mr. de Vere's mind is like his face, which seems to be *all eye & forehead;* not that it is disproportioned in size, but that the eyes & forehead alone fix the attention and seem to constitute the face. In Manning the countenance is positively unequal. He has an evanescent mouth,—which, as you pursue it, subsides almost into a nonentity—so that the face presents the form of a pear or a boy's top as you look at it from below the pulpit. There is a want of *mouth* to my mind in Manning's eloquent sermons; they are full of fine feeling put forth in a flow of heavenly-sounding language; but I think they want intellectual definiteness. Old sophisms, or such as have been challenged as such in modern argument, are reproduced without defences. A preacher may be quite justified in assuming the religious doctrines of his school, and announcing them as truths without defending them, but to reproduce old *arguments*, mere intellectualisms, without noticing the refutations, is to calculate on the ignorance of readers instead of appealing to their sense.

But all this is a digression from "The Triad," which some will defend by the example of "Lycidas." There is some difference between the scheme of "Lycidas" and that of the "Triad"; I have heard my Uncle Southey, adopting Johnson's criticism, observe of that exquisite poem, that it was very inappropriate as a lament for a young gentleman drowned in the Irish Channel in the year 16— In "Lycidas" poetic idealism is not brought so closely into contact & conflict with familiar reality as in "The Triad"; because it contains no description of the individual young gentleman himself. The theme in reality is quite general and abstract—death by drowning of the friend of a great Poet in his bloom of youth—a minister of the Gospel. This theme is adorned with all the pomp & garniture of classic & Hebraic imagery that could be clustered and cumulated around it. After all, in theory Milton's mixture of Pagan mythology with the spiritualities of the Gospel is not defensible: the best defence of "Lycidas" is not to defend the design of it at all, but to allege that the execution is *perfect*,—the diction the *ne plus ultra* of grace and loveliness, and that the spirit of the whole is as original as if the poem contained no traces of the author's acquaintance with ancient pastoral poetry from Theocritus downward.

I am much pleased to see how highly Mr Wordsworth speaks of Virgil's style and of his Bucolics, which I have ever thought most graceful and tender. They are quite another thing from Theocritus, however they may be based upon Theocritus.

Mr. H. C. Robinson was here this morning & talked of the Memoir of his beloved friend. He would have gone down upon his knees, he said, to prevent the biographer from including the paper of reminiscences at the end of Vol II. He thinks the remarks on Goethe really discreditable to his great friend; for Wordsworth knew hardly anything of Goethe's writings, and was not aware how great a similarity existed between his best strains of poetry and some of the best of his own. This similarity I had felt before Mr Robinson, who is well acquainted with modern German literature, & knew Goethe personally, pointed it out.

You invited me in a former letter to speak to you of "the Prelude"—but this must be reserved for a future communication. I can only say now, that I was deeply delighted in reading it, and think it a *truly noble* composition. It is not perhaps, except in certain passages, which had been extracted and given to the public before the publication of the poem as a whole, effective and brilliant poetry. But it is deeply interesting as the image of a great poetic mind; none but a mind on a great scale could have produced it. As a supplement to the poetic works of the author it is of the highest value. You may imagine how I was affected and gladdened by the warm tributes which it contains to my Father, and the proofs it affords of their close intimacy and earnest friendship. I think the history of literature hardly affords a parallel instance of entire union and unreserve between two poets. There may have been more co-operation between Beaumont & Fletcher, but from the character of their lives there could hardly have been such pure love, and consonancy of thought & feeling on high themes and accordance in high aims and endeavours.

Mr Yarnall's remembrances of the Poet in his last year I

thought highly interesting. I saw in them a touch of Wordsworth's own manner—a reverent tenderness and "solemn gloom." To judge from the notes of Mrs. Davy and Lady Richardson Mr W. must have been somewhat more like his old self in discourse when at his own home surrounded by the natural objects, in which he took such high interest, than when I was with him at Miss Fenwick's at Bath, in the spring of that sad summer which deprived him of his beloved daughter. Then he seemed unable to talk except in snatches and fragments, and there was nothing fresh in what he said. His speech seemed to me but a feeble mournful echo of his former utterances. He must have written more letters to you than to any one of late years. How much the biographer is obliged to you for inducing him to write so often on literary matters! The benefit to the world would have been great indeed had the Bard been a good letter-writer—but it is generally felt that his letters are not very good except when they are not letters at all—in their nature—but essays.

My cousin Cuthbert Southey has entered upon his new sphere of duty at Ardleigh in Essex under melancholy circumstances and in deeply depressed spirits. His amiable, long ailing wife was suddenly taken from him, some inward disorder being brought to a crisis apparently by influenza, last March; our aged Aunt, Mrs Lovell, who has lived with him ever since his marriage, has been so much weakened by the same complaint, that she is unable to journey from the North of England to the East. His sister—Kate Southey—who resides in an elegant & well situated cottage on the Vicarage hill at Keswick, cannot leave her and a faithful old servant, who also is too weak to move; and Cuthbert's four little children cannot be separated from their Aunt. Thus my poor cousin is obliged in the first bitter stage of his bereavement to reside at his new living quite alone, with no one familiar face either by his fireside or in his neighborhood, no lady friend or relative to manage his household and look after his domestic comforts. I trust however that his domestic happiness will have, if not a second *spring*, yet another season as satisfactory as the first has been, or more so; more untroubled if not more gladsome. The last two volumes of his book were better liked upon the whole than their predecessors. When he was with me he seemed, not depressed by the public reception of the Life & Correspondence, but sobered by it. He told me that the trouble and annoyance attendant on biographical undertakings outweighed to his mind, any advantages arising from them, and that he should be slow to take up the pen again in that way. His book was not kindly dealt with by that many headed monster, which for one human head has twenty bestial ones, of fox, wolf, ass and goose, hyena & hybrids of various kinds and proportions, *the Periodical Critical Press;* but I really think it will rise with time in general estimation rather than lose ground. Sir Robert Inglis spoke of it warmly to me the other day; and it is the opinion of my brother Derwent, and several other persons with whom I have lately talked, that it is a better performance than this of Dr Wordsworth; that the book of the two is better arranged, and the original parts more interesting, contributing something more toward a lively image of the man—the subject of the work. Mr. Wordsworth's old friend and early admirer, Mr Kenyon, (John Kenyon, author of several volumes of poetry, and a man of fortune)concurred in the general opinion of the Wordsworth Memoir—"heavy as a whole, though containing good materials." The specimens of the Poets literary criticism, which appear, rather tend to give a wrong notion of that department of his mind. He was highly instructive and entertaining in his remarks on writers of past ages & on the treatment of his popular contemporaries he was analytic [,] searching and severe, and, as many thought—many even of his own deep admirers—ungenial and almost narrow and unjust. Now all this part of his mind & temper is suppressed & Dr W. has thought fit to publish a few letters of civility & compliment to writers whose works he despised and which must sound to those who are intimately acquainted with his habits of criticism, who remember that he never spoke of Byron & Campbell except in censure of their thoughts & diction, denied all merit to Carlyle, and, regardless of his humor & pathos and power of word-painting represented him only as a charlatan and vitiator of the English language, that he not only decried Scott's poetry, but allowed little merit to his romances!—hollow & unnatural. There is a civil letter to R.M. whose poem he called "omnipresence of folly & nonsense." I have heard him rejoice that he had thanked the author for it before he had read it.

On the other hand he sometimes exalted persons, even intellectually, in whom the world could see nothing—indeed I must think he bestowed upon some, who had interested his fancy or affections in some peculiar way felt by himself alone, gifts and graces of his own creation. Mr. Peace, whom he honored with so much notice, may certainly have more in him than I can see, but he strikes me as a person of little judgment. This I thought when I met him at Bath & he has since rather confirmed the impression by issuing proposals for forming a monument to Mr W's memory by carving a mountain into his effigy. This notion of making a fool of a mountain—one of the Poet's beloved hills in order to do him honour—is worthy of Shallow or Slender—it is the fantastical prosaic mistaken for the poetical.

Perusal of the Memoir has revived & rather strengthened in me an opinion that there must be in John Wordsworth, the poets eldest son (now Mr Wordsworth) some small measure of poetic feeling and even expression-power akin to that of his Father—a slight leavening of the Wordsworthian genius, which has been almost stifled by sluggishness of temper. I judge this from his metrical Latin letter and some other indications; yet he passed for a dull boy—a *very* slow one he undoubtedly was; and he is still thought heavy in general society. He seems to inherit the temperament of his Uncle Capt John Wordsworth (not *from* him of course) the notices of whom in the Life are to me among the most interesting passages it contains. The Extracts from dear Miss Wordsworths Journal shew what a true Poet's helpmate she was. Never was a Poet so blest before in the ladies of his household. By the bye, how surprised I was to see two instances in which Mr. Wordsworth himself uses that vulgar, newspapery term—"females"—for women or ladies. I thought he condemned it, as my Uncle S. & my Father certainly did.

I am come to the end of my fourth or 3rd & a half sheet, and must turn to other tasks, and tax your eyes and attention no longer. Will you give my kind regards to Mrs. Reed. What a pleasure it would be to see you both in England and talk with you on subjects in which we take common interest! Believe me very faithfully and sincerely your friend

SARA COLERIDGE

I must tell you that on the relative merits of W's latest and other poetry, I am in accordance with C. H. Townshend and Thos. Blackburne both poets & widely acquainted with poetry; and that my Father and Mr Kenyon, I believe, held pretty much the same opinion. 'Spite of this you will agree with de Vere & Quillinan and think such views a sort of literary heresy. The Edinboro Article on my Uncle Southey's Life and writings among other blunders repeats the old calumny about my Father, which has been twice publicly refuted, that he left his children without provision.

The Poems of my brother Hartley have had a favourable reception from the public generally, but there is an *atrocious* article on the Life in the "Spectator." A friend of Hartley's who knew him well intends to answer it.

6

10 Chester Place
December 22 1851

My dear Professor Reed

Many weeks ago I heard from Mr Yarnall with deep concern of your severe, lingering illness—lingering, though transitory I trust, in its nature. A week since I received from your friend another long and very interesting letter, which conveyed to me the welcome news, that, though still confined to your bed, you were in a fair way of recovery. It may be premature to congratulate you on positive recovery—and Mrs. Reed with you; but I may say how hopefully I look forward to it, & how rejoiced I should be to hear of your restoration to your family and all your various activities, literary and professional.

Would that *my* health prospect were as yours—as hopeful! I am now an invalid confined to my own room and the adjoining apartment, with little prospect of restoration, though I am not entirely hopeless. My malady which had been threatening me ever since the summer before last, did not come into activity till a few months ago. What my course and the event may be—perhaps no physician can tell *to a certainty*. I endeavour not to speculate—to make the most of each day as it comes, making use of what powers remain to me, and feeling assured that strength will be supplied, if it be sought from above, to bear every trial which my Father in Heaven may think fit to send. I do not suffer *pain*. My principal suffering is the sense of sinking and depression. Of course all literary exertion & extensive correspondence are out of the question for me in my present condition. New editions of my Fathers works are in contemplation, and I can still be of use to my brother Derwent in helping to arrange them. But any *work* that I do now is of a very slight and slow description.

Mr. Herbert Taylor kindly offers to send to Philadelphia any book or pacquet for me, and I take the opportunity of sending you an enlarged engraving of Wilkie's sketch of my brother Hartley, in which you were so much interested, and the more, from a likeness you discerned in it to your son. My Brother's biographical work, "The Northern Worthies," is in the press, and great pleasure I have in reading the proof sheets, and perceiving how much more merit there is in these Lives than I ever knew them to possess before. Their chief interest consists in the accompanying criticisms & reflections. I feel sure you will like them exceedingly, though of course you may dissent from many of the opinions and sentiments expressed.

Farewell, my dear Sir. You have my sincere wishes and prayers for your entire restoration. I *may* not be able to answer any more letters from America,—a land in which I shall never cease to take an interest,—but I shall ever hear with pleasure of you and yours, as long as my powers of thought remain. Give my kind regards to Mrs. Reed and believe me yours with much esteem and sympathy.

SARA COLERIDGE.

Will you give my thanks to Mr Yarnall, when you next see him for two very interesting letters, which I have received from him since I was confined to my room, It is not in my power to answer them in all their interesting details, but I read them with great pleasure and *refreshment*. I request all my friends & correspondents not to speak much of my illness—as the subject depresses me. I wish to be taken away from the invalid room as far as possible—to accompany my friends in their ramblings in the face of nature,—Mr Y's description of Niagara, often as I have read descriptions of that world-famous fall, gave me a new delight—and I like to hear their views on religion, politics, morals, all subjects of general interest.

I entirely agree with Mr Yarnall in what he says respecting Quakers. I believe there is as much Christian excellence to be found in that sect, in proportion to its numbers, as in any portion of Christendom—as much of the moral spirit of the Gospel. What a pleasing portrait of a Quaker Sir Walter Scott has given in "Red gaunlet"!

I have been deeply interested and delighted with Dr Nitsch's letter to Ida Countess of Hahn Hahn, ("Babylon & Jerusalem") on her recent conversion to Rome & publication on the subject (["] From Babylon to Jerusalem.") In no other work have I ever seen the respective character of Romish &

Reformed Christianity so profoundly brought out. The subject is not treated theologically, but in its deep spiritual, moral and practical bearings. The description of the Church of Rome,—what it is that gives it so powerful a hold on the minds of men—of intelligent and spiritual men,—is so elevated, so *favourable*—that, as I read, I imagined myself listening to Aubrey de Vere, or some other eloquent zealous convert to Romanism setting forth the glories of "the one holy Catholic & Apostolical Church." The admissions respecting the defects of Protestantism are so large & candid, that no one can accuse the writer of entertaining low dry views respecting what a Church ought to be. When he takes up the defence of the Reformation, and exhibits the *grounds* on which the Reformer acted, when he displays the very heart & centre of the faith in Christ and the essence of all Religion, he satisfies my whole mind & spirit. It is my own very body of belief, which has been gradually developed within me by reflections, from year to year, brought out into relief. In such views as these have I lived, and in such views as these, spite of all attempts to convert me to Romanism, or to recommend Romano-Anglicanism in my eyes—I think to die. I fully believe that to join the Church of Rome may be to many a zealous convert the means of grace & added spirituality—that it may quicken in him all religious feelings and aspirations, and lead him to devote himself to the service of God as he never devoted himself before. So it may be with the *individual*—Yet I believe that the effect of the Romish system at large is most injurious to morals. My brother Judge Coleridge, last night, gave me some strong instances of its power to undermine good faith & honesty. The most honourable & upright man, when he has joined the Church of Rome, often thinks himself free in conscience to violate engagements formed previous to his conversion, for the benefit of our Church.

Truth & true Religion cannot be at variance. In answer to a remark of a correspondent of Mr Yarnall, who commented in a kindly & genial spirit on my strictures on *Tractarianism*, (which is certainly on the *wane* here, while it is in the *ascendant* with you)—let me say, that I have ever thought myself, & meant to be, a maintainer of *a* sacramental system, though not exactly *the* system taught in the "Tracts for the Times." I have endeavoured to maintain that view of baptismal regeneration, which is taught by our Anglican divines, when the relics of mediaeval mysticism, which lingered in the mind of Hooker & Jackson and even of Taylor, (who gives the wrong view, as I think, and the right also, for the reader's choice) had been cleared away. My notion of the *nature* & *office* of Baptism, given in the Essay explanatory of my father's Baptismal doctrine, appended to the "Aids to Reflection," is exactly the same as that of Waterland—(Thorndyke's view seems to be similar). If I differ at all from him (Waterland) it is respecting *terms*, not respecting *things* or ideas. What he calls *regeneration proper* (i. e. the grant or consignment of the Spirit to the soul) I believe to be regeneration in a secondary sense. What he calls *renovation*, I believe to be the true Scriptural *regeneration*, as I am sure it is the sense of St John, in his general Epistle (1 John III 9). and of St Paul (Rom. VIII, 14). Renovation, conversion, justification, the gift of Righteousness, regeneration—all are but different aspects or sides of one great blessed fact—the soul of Man raised above itself and gratified for heaven.? [*sic.*]

But I had *no thought of theology*, when I commenced this letter—only I could not remain quite silent under the imputation of not believing the sacramental system. My Father's idea of the Eucharist—his evolution of the Catholic idea—is given in his notes on Luther's Table Talk (Lit Remains III 41.) My "Examination of Waterland's Theory of Baptismal Regeneration" is the 2nd vol of the Aids—6th edit p. 195. I merely refer to it in defence of my orthodoxy, not as ascribing to it any power to persuade.

One more protest I must make against the conclusions of your friend's friends, (whose cordiality & intelligence however have delighted me.) "Coleridge's religion is not for the Poor." If Coleridge's *philosophy* of religion is not for the Poor —what *philosophy* can be? His *Christianity* was for Rich & Poor, Learned and Ignorant alike. He of all men in this age, perhaps, has done most to spread the conviction that Christianity is a *Life* not a set of propositions,—its seat in the *heart* not in the head—its *essence* not intellectualism but those spiritual ideas which are the common inheritance of all men.

I am pleased to hear that you are shocked by the "Life of Sterling." As a piece of *biography* it is interesting and affecting —biography is Carlyle's forte—but the work must open the eyes of many who, like myself, have felt unable to believe, without the author's own clear declaration, that a writer could go on, year after year, using the language of religious persons, while his heart discarded all which that language means, as "bottled moonshine."

Once more farewell. Prosperity be with you and yours.

When St John says "he who is born of God does not commit sin," of course we must take him to mean—is not *a sinner*— living in a *course of sin*? This is not contrary to what we must admit—that all men sin *more or less*. My interpretation is that of a host of eminent divines.

Dec. 27

I long to send you a copy of Dr Nitschs letter—but fear the little additional parcel should hurt the engraving.

I regret that in my letter I said a word about theology as such[.] It was not intended. Dr Nitschs letter is not theology but religion.

III

SARA COLERIDGE'S COMMENT ON HENRY REED'S *MEMOIR OF THOMAS GRAY*

III

MEMOIR OF GRAY

BY

PROFESSOR REED

p. 15. "Rather be the author of that poem than take Quebec."[1] This is indeed a most interesting anecdote. Query, is it characteristic of military men to be thus liberal and unappropriative? I certainly think no class of men are so antipathetic to poetry as men of science, mathematicians, and students of the particular sciences to which mathematics are applied. The wider study, which we call philosophy, the science of mind and of being, metaphysics at large, is not thus antagonistic to poetry, which it embraces in the compass of its analysis. A metaphysician like Kant is too knowing, too all-sided in knowledge to despise poetry, as a mere mathematician does. Plato's sentence upon poetry in the Republic has probably been misunderstood. Chemistry seems akin to poetry from the brilliant shews and curious combinations which it deals with & produces; it is full of sensuous matter for poetic thought. Davy poetized—though he was not *a poet*. I have heard Mr. Wordsworth say he might have been; but I think my Father, though he overflowed with love and admiration of Davy, would not have subscribed to that opinion. He thought W.W. too lavish in his attributions of poetic power in some directions, as he was generally considered too slow to allow it in others.

When in my girlhood I visited my brother Derwent at St John's College, Cambridge, with my dear mother, Professor Sedgwick shewed us the statue of Newton by Roubilliac, and I remember his expressing an opinion from which my young

[1]The allusion is to General Wolfe's celebrated remark about Gray's Elegy on the night before the battle of Quebec.

mind strongly dissented, that he was a far greater man than Milton. He knew far more of Newton's merits than I did,—but even then I *felt* Milton as many an able intelligent man can never do. And I doubt whether the powers and services of a philosopher like Newton cannot be far better estimated by one unlearned in mathematics and astronomy than those of the author of "Paradise Lost," by one who does not *understand* poetry. For the benefit of poetry is poetry itself,—both to the composer and the reader, it is its own exceeding rich reward.

p. 18. Eminent men, especially in literature, have often—that is many eminent men have owed more to their mother[1] than to their father, both for nature and education. It was so with Cowper, and with my Uncle Southey. But the truth, no doubt, is, that the parent whose mental qualities are most powerful and excellent most moulds the child that attains to eminence, whether it be father or mother, and when it happens to be the latter that is best endowed we are struck to find that man has derived less from man than from woman.

Seldom has a Poet had so poetical a son as S T Coleridge had in Hartley. Not one poet of this age beside has transmitted a spark of his fire to his offspring; but it is curious that Hartley excelled most in the sonnet, in which my father excelled least of all the poetic forms that he attempted.

p. 21. "A father's wrongs.[2]" Is not this a doubtful expression? But for what had gone before we should suppose wrongs *suffered by a father* to be meant. A *wrong* is not a wrongful thing done, but undergone, I *think*, in common parlance. "Your injuries"—is more ambiguous, [it would rather have

[1]"It was morever by that mother's unfailing fortitude and affection that the life thus saved was made fit for all that gave it happiness and honour. The father's character stands in dark contrast. . . . Philip Gray was an improvident, selfish, morose, and passionate man, the excesses of whose temper stopped not short of acts of brutal violence, which made him the terror of his household." *Memoir of Gray.*

[2]"Domestic discord, the knowledge and often the sight of conjugal cruelty and misery, a father's wrongs and a mother's sufferings, could not but affect a spirit naturally sensitive, with a gloom which the after years would never do away with." *Memoir of Gray.*

an active than a passive signification, if unexplained.[1]] Perhaps this is a wrong of mine, my active wrong to your style.

pp. 22, 23. All that you say[2] in these pages about the enduring benefit of early happiness and tranquillity is well said, and to my mind most true. I shall inclose a scrap[3] which I wrote a few weeks ago to the same effect, though mine is but a sketch and yours a picture. Edith spent three months this summer among the hills and streams, in sight of which my years of childhood and girlhood passed away—or passed into the married state which makes an end of girlishness, whenever it takes place. During that time I kept from her certain subjects of anxiety, which she could not but know on her return home; and very thankful I felt that it was in my power to keep the clouds from her sky which were darkening my own. It is good for children to be happy and cheerful; early sorrow weakens the mind, if it does not harden it, as premature disproportioned labour injures the body. I know this by experience and have carefully shielded my children's young minds from the troubles and constraints which so often came upon my own like frosts and wintry blasts on "the darlings of the Spring."

[1]The words in brackets are cancelled in the manuscript.

[2]"Gray felt the cruel wrong which robs childhood of the rightful property of its innocence, the happiness, which, in after-years too, comes again with its glad memories to soothe and cheer and refresh the severer condition of adult and even aged humanity. A cloud that hangs over early life casts a long shadow: it travels onward with the life, ever and anon, fitfully or habitually obscuring it with gloom and despondency,—a moodiness which is perhaps unconscious memory of the past." *Memoir of Gray.*

[3]The "scrap" reads as follows:

I think with my dear Uncle Southey, that we ought to shield our dear ones from trouble and sorrow as long and as much as we can. No fear of their not having sufficient discipline by what Life *will* bring in its course, let Love do what it may to make their sky all blue and their path all velvet.

I am sure it is good to be happy in our early years, when all happiness is more complete and intense, at least on its earthly side, than it can be, when the constitution is less joyous: to have the memory stored with bright remembrances and the nervous system saved from early shock & irritation. I should be a different creature now, perhaps, but for the mental agitations and disproportionate bodily exertions of my childhood and youth.

Therefore I do so rejoice that I took courage to let Edith travel to the North by herself—& that she extended her travels to Morpeth, Durham &c. I think you agree with me in these views.

N.B. I have not meant to insinuate that I was a darling of Spring except as all her children are darlings.

Aubrey de Vere, son of the late Sir Aubrey de Vere of Curra[g]h Chase, about 15 miles from Dublin, is the poetic friend of whom I spoke in the note at p 173 of the B.L. The expression "covered her over with day & night," or "spread day and night over her," is all I took literally from him,—indeed all that is worthy of notice in the note.

I have lived among Poets a great deal, and have known greater and better Poets than Aubrey de Vere—but a more *entire poet*—one more a poet in his whole mind and temper[a]-ment, I never knew or met with. He is *most amiable*, uniting a feminine gentleness and compassionateness with the most perfect manliness, both negative and positive. He is all simplicity—yet so graceful and gracious! A polished *Irish* gentleman is the most polished of all gentlemen—And Aubrey de Vere is such—sportive & jestful—yet with a depth of seriousness in his nature ever present. He is 6 foot 2—slender and graceful with a fair clear skin emblematic of the perfect purity of his mind. He is an intimate friend of Henry Taylor.

p. 30. Horace Walpole[1]

The oftener one meets Walpole in the region of Literary Biography, the more the impression is intensified, that he was a respectable Fribble, and a compact solid mass of frivolity and littleness—a marked specimen of the genus superficial &c. Poets are men of feeling *κατ'—ἐξοκην* [*sic*]. They are the soft rich peaches and he was the little hard winter pear, that leaves a dent in every one of the former with which it comes in contact.

p. 32. I should think Gray could never have written a philo-

[1] "After a residence of about a half year in his father's house, Gray, at the request of his friend and schoolmate, Horace Walpole, accompanied him on a continental tour, which occupied more than two years, spent chiefly in Italy. . . . At Reggio, in 1741, after two years of travelling companionship, Gray and Walpole parted, and in anger." *Memoir of Gray*.

sophic poem[1] under any circumstances. Mr de Vere used to talk of Tennyson's writing an Epic—No more than Milton could or would have written the "Lady of Shalott." People will next talk of Haynes Bailey producing a new "Hamlet." I do not believe that Keats would ever have written anything better or higher than he had already produced. The "Hyperion," so exalted by Shelley, is to my mind a falling off in felicitous originality. It is too Miltonic. Gray was a very *sensible* man, and self-knowing. His own remarks on the poetical habits which unfitted him for the production of a poem of large compass seem to me excellent and are just what I have often heard in other words from W.W. & H Taylor. There must be flat, rough spaces in an extensive domain if it is to be traversed with pleasure, and Gray could not be flat and rough like Dante. He had not masculine force enough for that. His verse, if not neat and polished, would have been nothing. Elegance and tenderness are its very soul.

p. 37. Something very candid in this account[2] of their differences. So like a poet to exaggerate the importance of the rupture—or seem to do so! My father was doing this sort of thing all his life long—and his great friend had quiet quarrels enough to fill a volume but *his* heart's hide was tougher than that of S.T.C. or R.S. The rupture did not break so much off from him. On his side the cliff was not so *scarred* and riven as on the opposite.

[1]The fragment, " 'De Principiis Cogitandi,' which is the most considerable of his Latin compositions, and far the most elaborate of all his poems in the conception. It was meant to stand in much the same relation to Locke's 'Essay on the Human Understanding' as Lucretius's poem 'De Natura Rerum,' did to the system of Epicurus." *Memoir of Gray.*

[2]"The rupture between Gray and Walpole appears to have an almost exaggerated importance in the poet's biography. . . . Indeed, with most men, such an occurrence would have passed away as one of the casual and most common disappointments of life,—the natural results of circumstances bringing into too close connection two uncongenial tempers. Yet, upon a spirit so delicately sensitive as Gray's, the effect was no doubt a deep and abiding one; it probably compelled a more recluse reserve and a more self-consuming silence, and thus aggravated the morbid tendencies of his nature." *Memoir of Gray.*

p. 40. "delicate hand writing.[1]"

It is remarkable what fine hands men of genius write, even when they are as awkward in all other uses of the hand as a cow with a musket.

p. 41. Do you think "Ion" a work of poetic genius[2], or only of an admirer of poetic genius? There was a want of poetic judgment in putting such intense Wordsworthian *modernism* into an ancient form, I thought, like drinking Barclay's entire out of an antique drinking vessel, meant to hold Chian or Falernian wine. "Ion" was of the same kind as the Düsseldorf reproductions of Raphael.

p. 46. Landor would be pleased at your compliment to his verse Latinity[3]. I have been wont to hear scholars say that his Latin verse had merit, but not that of *classicality*.

Last winter's number of the Ed Review contains an article on Landor's poetry by my friend, Mr Aubrey de Vere. The article contains an ingenious and eloquent comparison & contrast between the genius of ancient Greece and that of Catholic Christianity with reference to poetry and the arts. But it failed to inspire me with any warm admiration of the poetic productions of Landor. In him I had, as a girl, an *implicit* faith, induced upon me by my Uncle's attributions to the great self-assertor, whose most amiable trait, I must think is his cordial admiration of, & warm testimonies to, Robert Southey. Landor's criticism is very acute and refined. His dialogues I admire. But his poems appear to me cold and ineffective—the verse of a man too knowing and tasteful to write bad poetry, but without poetic genius to write well. At least such was the impression on my mind. Some few passages of Landor's poetry are striking.

[1]"Travellers have sought at the Grande Chartreuse for the original copy of the Ode in Gray's delicate handwriting, but in vain." *Memoir of Gray*.

[2]"And still less was he [Gray] equal to that combination of effort which in our own day, has given to Talfourd distinction both as a lawyer and a poet." *Memoir of Gray*.

[3]"It has been reserved for a living and now aged author, Walter Savage Landor, to acquire distinction by the exquisite beauty and classical purity of his Latin poetry, by his English poems, and still more by his admirable English prose." *Memoir of Gray*.

p. 49. I was a little disappointed that you did not notice here my Fathers notes on Gray's *Platonica*.[1] "Whatever might be expected from a scholar, a gentleman, a man of exquisite taste, as the quintessence of sane and sound good sense, Mr Gray appears to me to have performed. The poet Plato &c &c. But Plato the philosopher was not to be comprehended within the field of vision, or to be commanded by the fixed immovable telescope of Mr Locke's human understanding &c &c &c"

De Quincey ("the Opium Eater" as he undignifiedly calls himself) called Parr "a coarse old Savage," and whatever his scholarship might be would give him little credit, I believe, for any judgment on the internal merits of Plato.

p. 51. Ode to Eton College.[2]

My father criticises the stanza "Say Father Thames" as the "only very objectionable one in point of diction"—the worst ten lines he calls it in all the works of Mr Gray—"falsetto throughout, harsh and feeble." He also condemns

1 And envy wan &c
2 Grim-visaged &c
3 And sorrow's piercing dart

"as 1 bad in the first, 2 in the second, 3 in the last degree."

p. 55. How different the fate[3] of poor "Christabel" when she did appear! Enemies so fierce that even old friends seemed afraid to admire and protect her. I have heard her sneered at & Lord Byron's praise called flummery, by men who now would as soon think of sneering at Gray's Elegy as at the "wild and original poem."

[1]" 'To the works of Plato he [Gray] paid great attention, as may be seen in the extracts from the Pembroke MSS.' . . . In the estimation of the late Dr. Parr, Gray stood second among those whom he considered best acquainted with the philosophy of Plato." *Memoir of Gray*.

[2]"In 1747, the Ode to Eton College was published by Dodsley, being the first separate publication of any of Gray's productions." *Memoir of Gray*.

[3]" 'The Elegy' was much handed about in manuscript, and, like Coleridge's 'Christabel,' in that condition gained considerable celebrity." *Memoir of Gray*.

p. 56. I wonder what Dodsley's "pinches"[1] were. One would rather not have any particular locality for the Elegy, than have one assigned [,] I think.

Pp. 57, 58. The strain of *thought* in the Elegy would not have made it popular without the strain of verse,[2] the metrical accordance with the tone of feeling in the contents. But this metrical accordance is surely but the *causa sine qua non* of its general acceptability. The efficient cause—the peculiar merit—I have ever supposed to be that inexpressible felicity and delightfulness of diction of which the line noticed by Sir E Brydges

"The rude forefathers of the hamlet sleep"

is but one instance out of a host. Then the composition and combination of the sentiments and images—in *this* lies the charm—more than in the images themselves. These indeed were not new—scarce one but had been presented in poetry before.

It has been the fashion with admirers of Shelley & Keats to disparage Gray. I remember coming out bluntly to my poetical friend Mr de Vere with the opinion, that he looked coldly upon the author of the Elegy purely because he was simple and intelligible, and used the English language in the ordinary senses, not procuring for himself a *semblance* of the sub-

[1]To Walpole for his care of the publication of the Elegy, Gray wrote:
" 'You have, indeed, conducted with great decency my little *misfortune*. Nurse Dodsley has given it a pinch or two in the cradle, that (I doubt) it will bear the marks of as long as it lives.' The locality of the 'Elegy' is somewhat undetermined; but happily the interest of the poem is not at all dependent on such a question." *Memoir of Gray*.

[2]"Gray himself witnessed the sudden popularity of the poem with surprise, and is said to have attributed it to the subject, which might, he thought, have been as well received if written in prose as in verse. . . .'Gray's Elegy owes much of its popularity to its strain of verse' [writes Southey] . . . . If it be not an ungracious effort to analyze the fame of 'The Elegy,' it may be traced first to the universal and unfailing interest of its theme and the pensive beauty that envelops it; then to the manifold workings of a pure and cultivated imagination upon it; and, further, to an exquisite diction and the charm of the music of appropriate metre. 'I know not,' said Sir Egerton Brydges 'what there is of spell in the following simple line:

The rude forefathers of the hamlet sleep;

but no frequency of repetition can exhaust its touching charm.' "

Memoir of Gray.

lime by an easily assumed obscurity, and a mock magnificence by straining and inflection.

For the same reason Crabbe is undervalued by devotees of Tennyson. Yet his "Tales of the Hall" display an acquaintance with the finer shades of human character and the various phases and aspects of human sorrow, a vein of reflectiveness softened by poetic feeling, which render them a most interesting study to persons who have seen enough of Life as it is in all its strangeness & sadness, to recognise the truth and worth of his representations. I believe that Crabbe in his personal character had all that sympathy with suffering humanity which appears in his poems. Yesterday I read a private letter of his, in which he laments over the introduction of machinery—and yet allows for the necessity of the Employers to use agents that "do not eat and drink." His sympathy with both parties is remarkable. I believe he was a gentle-hearted creature.

p. 63. How stupid not to like "the Long Story"![1] Surely *that* might have been understood at once.

p. 67. "Not a wise remembrancer"[2]

It is sometimes a relief thus to *objectize* our ailments. It seems to cast them *out* from us and give us a sort of mastery over them. The dumb state of misery, when one dares not talk of it, is by far the worst[.] Then it seems to possess one's whole being. There is a comfort also in looking back and seeing what miseries one has gone through before and got beyond.

[1] "One of the incidents of the popularity of 'The Elegy' was Gray's acquaintance with his neighbours, Lady Cobham and Miss Speed, which prompted his attempt at humorous poetry, 'A Long Story,' opening with the clever description of the Elizabethan architecture of Stoke-Pogis House. . . . In one of his letters to Wharton, he says of this effusion: 'The verses you so kindly try to keep in countenance were wrote to divert that particular family, and succeeded accordingly; but being showed about in town, are not liked there at all.' " *Memoir of Gray*.

[2] "In his pocket-journal, besides a diary of the weather and a calendar of observations on natural history, he kept that kind of record which is not a wise remembrancer for one of nervous temperament and valetudinarian propensities, a regular account of the state of his health" *Memoir of Gray*.

p. 87. "Tour to the Lakes."[1] It is said Gray set the fashion of touring to the English Lakes in search of the picturesque. His horse block is still shewn near the Vicarage of Keswick on a hill overlooking Crosthwaite Churchyard where my Uncle & Aunt Southey's remains lie buried, with Skiddaw in front. A few paces from that horse block is the Lairbeck Cottage where dwells my cousin Kate Southey, my Uncle's youngest, unmarried daughter, a young woman of remarkable qualities—with more of her Father's temper and character in her than any of his other children. She has great courage, energy, fortitude—*and has needed them.*

p. 88. "Tintern Abbey"[2]

The "Lines on Tintern Abbey"—is in my opinion one of the finest strains of verse which this age has produced.

p. 89. "near Stough in Bucks"[3]

A misprint perhaps for Slough (pronounced Slow—the ow as in *how, now*[,]cow.) A well known place to me for from the station, when I have visited Eton, I have always been fetched by the little carriage of my cousin and brother-in-law, Edward Coleridge, who has now, for a quarter of a century, been a Master at Eton—one of the 9 or 10 masters. I visited him there before my marriage—and many a time while my boy, now at Balliol College, Oxford, was a pupil of his and of the school. Now he has been trying for the Lower Mastership, after serving so many years with eminent success, obtaining numberless Oxford triumphs for Eton, and the

[1]"In the autumn of 1769, Gray made his tour to the lakes of Cumberland and Westmoreland,—that beautiful region, then little known, even to his own countrymen, but which in later times has been the life-long home of great poets." *Memoir of Gray.*

[2]"In the summer of that year [1770] he made what he describes as 'a six weeks' ramble through five of the most beautiful counties in the kingdom,' in the course of which he viewed with especial delight the scenery of the river Wye, 'the sylvan Wye—the wanderer among the woods,' and the ruins of Tintern Abbey, and spent a short time at Oxford." *Memoir of Gray.*

[3]From Gray's will: "'First, I do desire that my body may be deposited in the vault, made by my late dear mother, in the churchyard of Stoke-Pogis, near Stough in Buckinghamshire, by her remains.'" *Memoir of Gray.*

Influentials are resolved to keep him out of the place because of his reforming views and efforts. They fear the Innovator—the shabby conservatives of gross dishonesty and injustice! They think the system will last their time, perhaps, but, I believe, if they live 20 years longer the old house will come down on them with a crash. It would be more honourable to leave it now and lend a hand to build a better or mend the old edifice.

pp. 94, 95. This disquisition[1] is very interesting. I think it is not sufficiently attended to that "what a man does is the measure of what he can do" from one cause or another.

p. 97. "High spirits take away mine"[2]

The quiet gladness of children always cheers me—but the hilarity and vigour of grown persons depress the weak & tremulous spirits. We are hurt by the want of sympathy, and the comparison is odious.

[1] "Another feeling will rise up, somewhat in the form of complaint, in the thought that Gray might have been a much greater poet,—that he ought to have achieved that higher order of reputation which is fame. . . . Speculations of this kind have something vain in them; for, unless the life be closed too early, or forced from its natural course by sadly adverse influences, it may be said, that what a man does is the measure of what he can do." *Memoir of Gray*. The assertion that "what a man does is the measure of what he can do," Reed defends at length, maintaining that Gray had not, in the dismal recollections of his father and in his quarrel with his youthful fellow traveller, cause of unhappiness sufficient to spoil his whole life of creative activity; that Spenser, Milton, Wordsworth, and Lamb rose above far greater discouragements.

[2] "He never learned a later poet's truer wisdom, that

A cheerful spirit is what the Muses love,
A soaring spirit is their prime delight.

Even before his health was impaired, he said (in 1758), 'High spirits and gaiety overpower me, and entirely take away mine.' " *Memoir of Gray*.

IV

SARA COLERIDGE'S MARGINALIA IN HENRY CRABB ROBINSON'S COPY OF THE *MEMOIRS OF WILLIAM WORDSWORTH*

"Mr. H. C. Robinson requested that I would use the pencil or pen freely on the margins of his copy [of *Memoirs of William Wordsworth*]. The more notes the better. I fear he will be greatly disappointed by what I have written, and I almost wish it rubbed out, it is so trifling & in some instances not to the purpose—as I fear the owner of the book will think."

Sara Coleridge. [*Cf.* Letter 5, p. 63, *supra.*]

IV

MEMOIRS OF WILLIAM WORDSWORTH, I

[On the inside of the front cover are the following references to pages:]

166 n = abo^{t} the first public^{n}		By Mrs. H.N.C
		p 44
		99
		119
		207
		216
		220
	not read	260
		265
		270,1,2,4
		284,6,8,9 &c
		290
		308
		367,8,9
		380 to 3
		404
		421
	to read	427,30–3
		438
		446
		450
		452

[The above annotations, "not read" and "to read," are of uncertain significance, probably memoranda employed by Mrs. Coleridge as she perused the book. In the MS. the first is opposite a bracket including 260–270; the second is opposite another and overlapping bracket including 265–452.]

Pages 44-45, Mem.

S. C. [General comment on the *Memoirs.*] Lady Palgrave, though keenly interested in this book longs for more personal particulars—She would have had fewer pedigrees—more personalities.

Such remarks are continually made upon biographies. But the truth [is] the poor biographer gives what he has to give, and these facts of domestic life and business unless they are journalized from day to day are not accurately remembered. Even in our own life, as we look back, we see events huddled and massed together in a misty maze. This is still more the case when the biographer is of a younger generation than the subject.

Page 99, Mem. [Dorothy Wordsworth's first impression of Coleridge.] "At first I thought him very plain, that is, for about three minutes: he is pale, thin,* has a wide mouth, thick lips, and not very good teeth, longish, loose-growing, half-curling, rough, black hair" (in both these respects a striking contrast to his friend Wordsworth, who in his youth had beautiful teeth† and light brown hair).

S. C. *["pale," "thin," and "beautiful" underscored.] I am surprised at "pale," still more at "thin." I thought my father had been rather fleshy always & like myself in youth, only pale at times.

†I am sure they came of [on?] this & interchanged tooth character. My Father had greatly the advantage of teeth in my remembrance of the two.

Mem. "After tea he [Coleridge] repeated to us two acts and a half of his tragedy, 'Osorio.' "

S. C. "Osorio" was afterwards "Remorse."

Page 118, Mem. If also, as is not improbable, he [the reflecting reader] should be of opinion, that a "worshipper of nature'' is in danger of divinizing the creation and of dishonouring the Creator, and that, therefore, some portions of this poem might be perverted to serve the purposes of a popular and pantheistic philosophy, he will remember that the author of the *Lines on Tintern Abbey*, composed also the *Evening Voluntaries*, and that he who professes himself an ardent votary of nature, has explained the sense in which he wishes these words to be understood, by saying, that

''By grace divine,
Not otherwise, O Nature, we are thine.''

S. C. Parsonic and High Churchy! As if the glorious Lines on Tintern needed the apology & protection of the Evening Voluntaries!!

Page 119, Mem. [Comment on Peter Bell, who ''had a dozen wedded wives.''] ''The number of Peter's wives was taken from the trespasses, in this way, of a lawless creature who lived in the county of Durham, and used to be attended by many women, sometimes not less than half a dozen, as disorderly as himself; and a story went in the country, that he had been heard to say while they were quarrelling, 'Why can't you be quiet, there's none so many of you.' ''

S. C. Our old Wilsy of Greta Hall used to repeat this saying of an old dame who had 30 cats. ''Can't ye 'gree? There's nin sae many on ye!''

Page 125, Mem. At this period he [Wordsworth] entertained little reverence for ancient institutions, as such; and he felt little sympathy with the higher classes of society.

S. C. [Doubly lined in the margin, without comment.]

Page 126, Mem.

I've measured it from side to side,
'Tis three feet long, and two feet wide.

S. C. [Comment is confined to a single word:] dramatic

Page 128, Mem. "We dined with Mr. Klopstock, and had the pleasure of meeting his brother, the Poet, a venerable old man retaining the liveliness of youth."

S. C. [Opposite "venerable old man" is the query:] ?his age

Page 174, Mem. "I [Wordsworth] am for the most part uncertain about my success in *altering* poems."

S. C. [The words "about my success in *altering* poems," are underscored.] He well might be.

Page 207, Mem. "Coleridge was at that time in bad spirits, and somewhat too much in love with his own dejection, and he departed from us, as is recorded in my sister's journal, soon after we left Loch Lomond."

S. C. [The words, "much in love with his own dejection," are underscored, and starred in the margin]. My father gave a different account of this matter, & the cause of his departure, so far coincident indeed that his state of health made him sensitive to the cause as he might not have been otherwise.

Page 216, Mem. "These lines recurred to Wm's memory; and while he and I were talking of Burns, and the propsect he must have had, perhaps from his own door, of Skiddaw and his companions, we indulged ourselves in fancying that we might have been personally known to each other, and he have looked upon those objects with more pleasure for our sakes."

S. C. It was pleasant to me once to find, in talking with Mr. Carlyle, that he and I, when children, and in youth, had looked upon the same hills, he on the Scotch side and I on the English.

Page 217, Mem. "This mansion is indeed very large; but to us it appeared like a gathering together of little things."

S. C. So I felt at Trentham the Duke of Sutherland's.

Page 220, Mem. "A lady and gentleman, more expeditious tourists than we, came to the spot; they left us at the seat, and we found them again at another station above the Falls. C., who is always good-natured enough to enter into conversation with anybody whom he meets in his way, began to talk with the gentleman, who observed that it was a '*majestic* waterfall.' C. was delighted with the accuracy of the epithet, particularly as he had been settling in his own mind the precise meaning of the words grand, majestic, sublime, &c., and had discussed the subject with Wm. at some length the day before. 'Yes, sir,' said C., 'it *is* a majestic waterfall.' 'Sublime and beautiful,' replied his friend. Poor C. could make no answer; and, not very desirous to continue the conversation, soon came to us, and related the circumstance, laughing heartily."

S. C. This story has been told another way. "Yes Sir! majestic, and *very pretty*!" has said to have been the rejoiner of my Father's nice chuser of an epithet. N B [Perhaps referring to her notes on the fly-leaf at the end of the volume, where she writes for p. 220: Heard f. relate this, with exagerations [*sic*] —five or six epithets.]

Pages 259-260, Mem. Coleridge's health required change of climate; and, instead of taking up his abode in a glen in Cumberland, he was soon to be a voyager on the wide sea, and, after he had traversed it, to be enjoying the warmer breezes of the valleys of Sicily, and of the terraces and gardens of Malta.

S. C. Most pernicious were those warmer breezes to my Father. They excited him at first, but soon aggravated his constitutional ailments. At Malta he became confirmed in the opiumizing habit. The climate of Southern Italy is most injurious to persons whose nervous system requires to be braced and suffers from relaxation, being too relaxed in itself.

Page 260, Mem. If Providence had not blessed him [Wordsworth] with a wife, a sister, a wife's sister, and a daughter, whose lives were bound up in his life, as his was in theirs, and who felt,—what the world was slow in admitting,—that his poems were destined for immortality, and that it was no small privilege to be instrumental in conveying them to posterity, it is probable that many of his verses, muttered by him on the roads, or on the hills, or on the terrace-walks of his own garden, would have been scattered to the winds.

S. C. I doubt that. He would have acquired more pen ease and dexterity. I cannot however quite judge as to the nervous affection which writing produced.

Page 261, Mem. [Letter to Sir George Beaumont from Wordsworth, in which he apologizes for and explains a delay of eight weeks in writing to express his thanks for a favor.]

S. C. The strain of this letter reminds me of a vindication of his diligence and industry which I have heard the Poet make when one of the ladies boasted of having risen long before him. "Indeed, but I was up in my mind long enough before any one in the house."

Pages 264-265, Mem. Sir George, with a painter's eye, had remarked the beauties of that circular pool on Loughrigg which had been compared to the Italian Lake of Nemi, the *Speculum Dianæ*.

S. C. Turner's view of this lake in water-colour, in possession of Mr. Windus, is a fairy scene and appears ideal. The lake is far deeper, surrounded by higher rocks than Loughrigg Tarn. It lies at the bottom of a deep dell.

Page 271, Mem. Lady Beaumont.

S. C. Lady B's name was Margaret.

Mem. [Note] Dora Wordsworth, born Aug. 16, 1804.

S. C. She was christened Dorothy. We did not begin to call her Dora till she was past childhood, early childhood certainly.

Page 272, *Mem.* "Mr. Malone, in the account prefixed to the Discourses, tells us that Sir Joshua generally passed the time from eleven till four every day in portrait-painting. This it was that grieved me, as a sacrifice of great things to little ones."

S. C. Mr W. & my Uncle S. could not but regret Scotts want of devotion to literature for its own sake—for its humanizing influences—his using it merely as means to a further end, far less important.

Page 274, *Mem.* "You will, perhaps, think it is a strange fault that I am going to find with it, considering the acknowledged taste of the owner, viz. that, small as it is compared with hundreds of places, the domain is too extensive for the character of the country."

S. C. This is eminently the case with the flower-garden at Trentham: 20 acres. It looks like a huge flower factory or nursery.

Page 284, *Mem.* [Nearly all of the page is lined in the margin. The following remark by John Wordsworth is doubly and heavily lined in the margin with S. C.'s remark opposite:] "As for the 'Lyrical Ballads,' *I do not give myself the smallest concern about them.* . . . I am certain they must sell."

S. C. Capital! This is no mere brother's partiality. The tone is of one who *sees* what he speaks of with such certainty.

Pages 284-286, *Mem.* It is interesting and instructive to contrast such language as this, proceeding from the pen of an East India captain, who had been sent to sea when a boy, with the verdicts pronounced on the same subject at the same time by literary censors of high reputation, by whom the public consented to be guided, and who, for the most part, derided the "Lyrical Ballads" as idle puerilities, and treated their author with disdain, and his readers with pity. . . .

In the Poem on the "Fir-Grove," Wordsworth expresses a hope that the day would come when his brother would return to the Vale of Grasmere, and to the quiet cottage.

S. C. These little notices of Capt. W. are *highly* interesting. The Poem about the Fir grove is one of W's best and most Wordsworthian Poems; full of his head and his heart. But in youth one quietly absorbs the fine poetry around and about one; if one is receptive of such matter, as one does the perfuse air of Spring, without inquiring much *about* it. We begin to be *poetical* long before we begin to be *literary*. I think of many things now connected with Mr W's & my Uncle's & Fathers life and poems & marvel that I did not gain information concerning them. Experience comes too late and when we cannot use it for the most part in this life. We seem to be "baptized for the dead"—accomplished for the grave, instructed for the night when there is no execution—no work to be done by the direction of a wise well furnished mind.

Page 289, Mem. "We have had no tidings of Coleridge. I tremble for the moment when he is to hear of my brother's death; it will distress him to the heart,—and his poor body cannot bear sorrow."

S. C. I believe it was on hearing of Capt. W's death that my Father retired from company & fainted. I have heard the story of him; it was on hearing the death of some friend, and I think this was Capt. John Wordsworth.

This brother of Mr W. was thought heavy & commonplace by general observers.

Page 291, Mem. "Some of the newspapers carelessly asserted that he did not wish to survive his ship. This is false. He was heard by one of the surviving officers giving orders, with all possible calmness, a very little before the ship went down; and when he could remain at his post no longer, then, and not till then he attempted to save himself."

S. C. I have heard it said that Capt W. was perfectly stupified when the danger came upon him & incapable of exertion. This was probably false. But his shyness & taciturnity evidenced a something peculiar in his nervous system.

Page 293, Mem. "So good must be better; so high must be destined to be higher."

S. C. [Double-lined in the margin.]

Page 308, Mem. "It is the place, I believe, where that illustrious and most extraordinary man, Beaumont the Poet, and his brother, were born. One is astonished when one thinks of that man having been only eight-and-twenty years of age, for I believe he was no more, when he died. Shakespeare, we are told, had scarcely written a single play at that age."

S. C. [The words, "a single play at that age," are underscored.] A mistake. Shakespeare had certainly written R. & Juliet at that age and I believe Richard II.

Pages 309-310, Mem. [Wordsworth in a letter to Sir George Beaumont.] "Let me thank you . . . for your most acceptable present of Coleridge's portrait, welcome in itself, and more so as coming from you. It is as good a resemblance as I expect to see of Coleridge, taking it all together, for I consider C.'s as a face absolutely impracticable. Mrs. Wordsworth was overjoyed at the sight of the print, Dorothy and I much pleased."

S. C. I suppose this was the print from Northcotes picture. Mr. Richmond thinks there is power about the mouth and that it has more merit than has been generally allowed it. Allston's portrait is the best that has been taken of my Father. That by Phillips has his social look, but very little of his intellect. It is a gentlemanly picture. The copy which Mr Murray has is inferior to the original at Salston House near Ottery.

Page 367, Mem. Dorothy, or (as she is called in her father's poems, and as she was known to all around her) Dora, born August 16, 1804; the birth-day, also, of her mother.

S. C. Dora was a picturesque and, I believe, a beautiful child at six years old, with long yellow locks, which her Father used to call "angelic hair." I remember Miss W. & my Father asking me if she was not a lovely little girl, when I was myself but 8 years old or hardly that. I replied bluntly—"No." I could not appreciate the picturesque, and thought my white-skinned cousin Edith a thousand times prettier—indeed quite a model of beauty. Mr W. was not so fond of Dora in her middle childhood as when she was approaching woman's height. Then he began to idolize her—to see in her genius and beauty, though all of a special sort. But she was not beautiful after childhood. In her teens, especially the earlier ones she had fine hair, a full face and a good colour, an unlovely mouth & eyes finely set in the head with a shapely espiégle figure. I remember how well she looked in a habit with her slim waist. She improved in countenance and manner as she worsened in mere corporeal appearance. Early in life she lost bloom & became liny, and in some respects old-looking. So she struck strangers from 25 onward. But she was ever much admired as well as loved, and was one of the most interesting women I have ever known. Her warmth of heart was her great charm. She was all tenderness and attention to others & self-postponement. For years when she was a child Dora's hair remained uncut, and the keeping it curled was a trobblesome [*sic*] & not always sightly affair. She was wild & ungovernable as a young one—but ever most affectionate.

Pages 379-81, Mem. [These pages contain an account of the deaths of two of Wordsworth's children: Catharine, June 4, 1812; and Thomas, December 1 of the same year.] The feelings of her [Catharine's] father at this sad loss are expressed in one of his sonnets [according to footnote, "Surprised by Joy"]. Suggestions of comfort are presented to his mind in another poem [according to footnote, "Desponding Father"].

S. C. Little Tom was pale & light-haired—slow in learning, at least when I had the opportunity of observing him. He spent some weeks at Greta hall and grew so fond of our old Wilsy that he cried bitterly, when taken away, and it was only by force that he could be removed from her side. "I want to stay with Wilsy," he cried most piteously. His Father, I think, was annoyed. Entre nous—the dear Ws did not make children comfortable and delicate children felt their rough management painfully.

I cannot think "Desponding Father" refers to loss of children. It plainly speaks of sorrow at the development of certain dispositions in sons.

"Nor fret thou
At like unlovely process in the May
Of human life"—

Poor little Katy Wordsworth was paralytic from her infancy. She was first struck when a babe in the nurse's arms after eating raw carrot, which the servant imprudently had suffered her to swallow. Mr. Dequincey[1] was extremely fond of her when she was about three years old—but in the eyes of people in general she was a plain, dull, ungainly child.

I have often wondered what loss is spoken of in that affecting sonnet "Surprised by joy" & never for a moment connected it with little Katy or imagined her capable of calling forth such a strain or being the object of it. She used to call me "Mr Coleridge's leetle girl" in a very slow drawling manner. I remember her mother's deep grief at her death. Mr W. seemed more afflicted at the death of Tom. How well I remember the poor child, going in a heart-broken way along the Forge Field, & beginning to still his sobs and submit to his fate toward the far end. He was a harmless mild boy when at K. and afterwards, we were told, opened out and improved very much before his death. Such was the father's tale.

[1]*Cf.* DeQuincey's account of little Kate's death and his deep sorrow thereat. *Collected Writings*. Ed. by D. Masson, II, 441–5.

Page 382, *Mem.* "THE FRIEND," by Coleridge, who *dictated* it (for he did not write it with his own hand) under Wordsworth's roof.

S. C. Miss Hutchinson kindly wrote for my Father in her beautiful hand. He was fondly attached to her and used to admire her long lightish brown hair. I remember his talking about it to me when I was a child. He was afterwards very fond of Mrs. Morgan & Miss Brent and still more perhaps of Mrs. Gillman.

Pages 403-4, *Mem.* "Now a country may advance, for some time, in this course with apparent profit: these accommodations, by zealous encouragement, may be attained; and still the Peasant or Artisan, their master, be a slave in mind, a slave rendered even more abject by the very tenure under which these possessions are held; and, if they veil from us this fact, or reconcile us to it, they are worse than worthless."

S. C. [First six lines of p. 404 are marked in margin.] Apply this to Lombardy under the Austrian yoke—as if that could be a paternal government which kept the mind in bondage. S T C's Letters on the Spaniards are full of fervid eloquence as well as solid reasoning. They might have been referred to here.

Page 408, *Mem.* "that pure air and purpurial sunshine,"

S. C. [Mrs. C. corrects the spelling of purpurial (purpureal).]

Page 420, *Mem.* [The end of Wordsworth's long letter to Sir C. Pasley].

S. C. A noble letter!

Mem. The following was written by Mr. Wordsworth, in the year 1840, to his friend, Professor Reed, of Philadelphia.

S. C. Professor Reed is now bringing out an edition of Wordsworths poems, in which he has done me the honour to introduce some of my little critiques. I must answer his last long & interesting letter tomorrow. His edition and Memoir of Gray are very creditable to his taste and literary accomplishments.

Page 427, Mem. "If, lastly, the motions of the soul transcend in worth those of the animal functions, nay, give to them their sole value; then truly are there such powers: and the image of the dying taper may be recalled and contemplated, though with no sadness in the nerves, no disposition to tears, no unconquerable sighs, yet with a melancholy in the soul, a sinking inward into ourselves from thought to thought, a steady remonstrance and a high resolve."

S. C. [The words, "dying taper," are underscored.] That affecting passage[1] about the taper should have been quoted.

Page 430, Mem. "And by this process, humility and docile dispositions may exist towards the master, endued as he is with the power which personal presence confers; but at the same time they will be liable to overstep their due bounds, and to degenerate into passiveness and prostration of mind. This, towards him; while, with respect to other living men, nay, even to the mighty spirits of past times, there may be associated with such weakness a want of modesty and humility. Insensibly may steal in presumption, and a habit of sitting in judgment in cases where no sentiment ought to have existed but diffidence or veneration."

S. C. How this was exemplified in the disciples of Newman —who learned in a lump ancient Fathers whom they had never read and to despise some of the greatest men the world ever saw from narrow and one-sided considerations!

Page 432, Mem. [This page contains the end of Wordsworth's reply to Mathetes in Coleridge's *The Friend*, Nos. 17 and 20.

[1]A reference to the first part of the paragraph, omitted in the *Memoirs*. *Cf. The Prose Works of William Wordsworth*, ed. by A. B. Grosart, I, 319.

The letter by Wordsworth, signed M.M., and in his Prose Works entitled *Advice to the Young*, is a good specimen of the Poet's prose style.]

S. C. Mr. W's prose style is very grand & perfect in its way. Perhaps my Fathers, even when equally elevated, as at the conclusion of the friend, has more ease—more Greek-like flow and naturalness—is more properly prose as distinct from poetry.

Page 438, *Mem.* The character of a deceased friend is not seen, no, nor ought to be seen, otherwise than through a tender haze or luminous mist that spiritualizes and beautifies it.[1] Such an epitaph is written by truth hallowed by love, the joint offspring of the worth of the dead, and the affections of the living.

S. C. Here comes an exquisite image of the ash-tree shone thro' & glorified by the evening sun. I doubt however the fitness of these long extracts and literary analyses in Memoirs. Mr Mackintosh intersperses his Father's Life[2] in the same way most profusely with passages from his writings and sketches of his works, abstracts of Lectures &c. One looks for something else in biography—to be told of the man, not to have to study the author. Allusions to the works and information about them are quite in place.

Page 446, *Mem.* In the year 1810, appeared a folio volume, entitled "Select Views in Cumberland, Westmoreland, and Lancashire," by the Rev. Joseph Wilkinson, Rector of East and West Wrotham, Norfolk.

S. C. This gentleman was married to a niece of the scientific Dr Brownrigg[3]—a friend of Herschel, who lived at Orma-

[1]This passage is quoted loosely by Christopher Wordsworth in the *Memoirs*. Wordsworth wrote: "otherwise than as a tree through a tender haze or luminous mist, that spiritualizes and beautifies it." Mrs. Coleridge apparently has the image of the tree confused with some other image.

[2]*Memoirs of the Life of the Right Honourable Sir James Mackintosh*. Ed. by his Son Robert James Mackintosh. London, Moxon, 1835.

[3]William Brownrigg, M.D. (1711–1800), an eminent Cumberland physician and chemist.

thwaite under Skiddaw: and at what had been his house they lived in my infancy. Mrs. W. a beautiful woman, superior in sense and refinement to her husband, was intimate with my parents, & was my godmother. She had been attached to Mr. Law,[1] who became Lord E. I believe, and for ten years continued to trust to his faith till she read his marriage in the newspaper and accepted Mr W's hand in a sort of despair.

Pages 446-447, *Mem*. Bishop Burnet, in his Tour speaks only of the *horror* of the Alps. Even John Evelyn appears to shudder at them. Even Goldsmith never dreamed of any such thing as beauty in them.

S. C. So Cotton in his continuation of Isaac Walton or second Part, talks of the *ugly* rocks and rough places of Derbyshire, Matlock &c.

Page 450, *Mem*. The form of a *Lake*, it is remarked, is then most perfect, when it least resembles a *river;* and when consequently, it inspires that placid feeling of repose, which particularly belongs to a lake as distinguished from a flowing stream.

S. C. Or from the sea. It is quieter than a river, more cheerful than the ocean, which is restless, often bleak and unreposeful from its unboundedness.

Page 452, *Mem*. [A discussion of the beauties of the Lake Country ascribable to the hand of man.]

S. C. The cottages in Easedale are specially exquisite in their tint. The vivid verdure of that vale, the whiteness of his foamy waterfalls and dashing streamlets with the greenish grey of its [*sic*] habitations form a lovely combination of hues. I should have mentioned also the colour of the rocks browner than the houses, and the purple of the hills in certain states of atmosphere. I do not remember however that it had the orna-

[1]Edward Law (1750–1818), who in 1802 became first Baron Ellenborough of Ellenborough in the County of Cumberland.

ment of golden furze so beautiful on the brow of Skiddaw mingled with violet heath, or the fern which fades into a fine ferrugineous or philamort colour in Autumn. The cottages of Borodale, especially in Stonethwaite, were of a blacker more earthy hue than those of Easedale.

Page 456, *Mem.* If I may be allowed the expression, it was as a priest of this *natural* temple, that the Poet came forward, and stood, as it were, at the threshold and deprecated an invasion of the sanctuary.

S. C. [This passage is heavily double-lined in the margin.]

Page 457, *Mem.* [This page continues the defence of Wordsworth's opposition to the Kendal and Windermere railway.]

S. C. [The first ten lines are marked in the margin.]

[On the yellow fly-leaf next to the back cover Mrs. Coleridge has entered brief notes with respective page numbers, probably intending to expand some of them in the text later. Her exact purpose, however, is open to conjecture. Written faintly in pencil, some of these notes have become blurred, and here and there a few words are illegible. The editor has endeavored to reproduce them as they were written.]

47 Qy the correctness
89 Ws religious feelings
p 118 Remark- Blake- Panthm- W's own remark
125 W. retained this feeling of love for the people
128 He lost his French
131 Schlegel also despised the pathetic
134 Mrs Barba[uld] Crabbe
163 Mrs Barbauld- to inquire
— For [?]— Letter to— The publication of it—
192 To whom written?
206 Compare with my note in Vol of poems
208 Why not publish Miss W's Journal?
212 Say who Hatfield was
220 Heard f. relate this, with exagerations[*sic*]- five or six epithets
268 dele[te] the he from the lines
269 Davy—Who?
276 Tiecks exclamation
280 Correct the mistake
330 Qy the wisdom of silence Talfourd & Ed Rev. Jeffry [*sic*]
334 Moods of my own mind—Why omitted? praise the headings
358 Two Voices are there Ws anecdote

[On the same fly-leaf below the notes given above are briefer notes or references, an imperfect index of Mrs. Coleridge's notes in the volume:]

Notes 44—Anecdotes
99 Coleridges teeth
118 Lines on Tintern
119 Cats. numerous
174 altering poems
207 Coler. in Scotland
216
217
220 epithets
260 Coler. health & industry
265 Loughrig Tarn
271
272 W. Scotts motives
274 Foxley
284 Capt. W
289, 290 } D°
308 Shakespeares age
309 Cs portraits
367,8 Dora in childhood
380 1,2 Tom & Kate W—
— Cs attachments
404 Austrian governmt
Cs letter on the Spaniards
420 Letter to Sir J Paisley [*sic*]
Professor Read [*sic*] of America
427
430
432 Ws prose style
438 Extracts from Words in biography
446 Mrs Wilkinson
ugly rocks
450 beauty of the lake
452 Easedale scenery

MEMOIRS OF WILLIAM WORDSWORTH, II

[On the inside of the front cover of Vol. II are the following references to pages:]

Hints
p 23
52
112
437

MS Notes by
S. C.
41
142 Rom. Cath
150–2 Do
157} family
159} feelings
162 Gr-
Lady B-
To read 182
189–91
355
mostly 359
unread 384 Emerson & Carlyle
motives for publishing 416, 7
Mesmerism 454
465 Milton
466

Page 28, Mem. The Brownie's Cell, suggested by a beautiful ruin on one of the islands of Loch Lomond.

Cora Linn, in sight of Wallace Tower.

S. C. [A check mark is opposite *The Brownie's Cell,* and *Cora Linn.*]

Page 41, Mem. "Accordingly, I resolved to plant yew-trees in the church-yard."

S. C. This is mentioned for the third time.

Page 52, Mem. It extorted from Southey the well-known saying uttered on hearing that a certain celebrated critic was boasting that he had "*crushed* 'The Excursion.'"

S. C. Jeffery [*sic*]

Page 112, Mem. In Sonnet xxx. p. 73. of the *first* edition of the "Ecclesiastical Sketches."

S. C. [Passage is checked in the margin.]

Page 143, Mem. In all the reasonings of the friends to this bribing scheme [the proposal to take the Romish Church in Ireland into pay] the distinctive character of the Papal Church is overlooked. . . . I agree with those who deem it probable that through a natural and reasonable desire to have their property duly represented, many landholders who are now Protestants will be tempted to go over to Popery.

S. C. Is not this taking the matter by a wrong handle? If the Romish Priest, or even the Romanist Layman, can be a good subject to a Protestant Monarchy at all, the Priesthood of Ireland may be so in spite of a government stipend. Their poverty now leads them to disaffection, turbulence, and ambition as W. himself shews in the next paragraph.

Pages 150-153, Mem. [Comment at the close of Wordsworth's long letter to an unknown Lord, on the Church of Rome, dated March 3, 1829.]

S. C. Mr Q. is displeased at the publication of this admirable letter; but what excuse can there be for supressing one of the most elaborate and carefully composed letters that W. ever wrote, and which contains a clear full account of opinions and display of sentiments perfectly consistent with the general frame of his mind & thoughts throughout his whole life, and which in the form in which they appear in the letter, occupied his mind for many years, and were never in any degree abated or in any particular modified? His biographer was *bound* to present so characteristic a part of his mind.

After all, whatever Q. may himself think, he cannot deny the fact, that many wise, learned, thoughtful good & pious men, and persons well informed both in the theory and practice of Romanism, do take just the same view of it, that Mr W. expresses in this powerful letter. Why is not the name of the person addressed given?

Page 153, Mem. "By reason of my having passed at least three years of life in countries where Romanism was the prevailing or exclusive religion; and if we are to trust the declaration 'By their fruits ye shall know them,' I have stronger reasons, in the privilege I have named, for passing a severe condemnation upon leading parts of their faith, and courses of their practice, than others who have never been eye-witnesses of the evils to which I allude."

S. C. [These lines are marked in the margin.]

S. C. [At the bottom of the page is this brief note]; NB W conv.^{er} with W. D Arnold

Page 155, Mem.
S. C. [Lines 11–17 are marked in the margin.]

Page 156, Mem.
S. C. [Lines 4–7 are marked in the margin.]

Page 157, Mem. [Comment in a letter to G. H. Gordon on *The Triad.*] "It had been promised several years to two of the party before a fancy fit for the performance struck me; it was then thrown off rapidly, and afterwards revised with care."

S. C. Edith Southey begged Mr W. to write a poem about us three. I knew nothing about it till it came forth. Though more interested in Mr W's poetry in general than Edith or perhaps even than Dora—more than Dora would have been but for her tie to the Poet.

[This note, without further suggestion in the text, is continued on pages 158–159.] I was oftener and longer at Rydal Mount than my cousin, & listened far more to the great Poets discourse. Yet the contrary would be inferred from these volumes—so many notices of Edith—not one of me in connection with W. and Miss Wordsworth. No notice too of my brothers intimacy with the Wordsworth family & constant intercourse with them.

Page 162, Mem. Mr. Wordsworth's dear friend Sir George Beaumont had departed this life on the 7th February, 1827, and was soon followed by his widow, Lady Beaumont, who died 14th July, 1829. . . . "When I sat down in Lady Beaumont's grotto, near the fountain, I was suddenly overcome, and could not speak for tears."

S. C. N B—Lady Beaumont had been a great beauty in youth and at 70 years old she was a proof that there may be great beauty in age both of form and colour in the human countenance. Her skin was white, her eyes were large black and liquid, they seemed to swim in silvery light and her features had much grace and dignity. This was physical comeliness—her expression not being remarkable. Her figure was not fine and her manners wanted the grace and courtesy by which those of her husband were distinguished. She was simple-minded and benevolent but not very refined in feeling and intellect, and was apt to descant authoritatively, at second hand upon subjects of art & poetry upon which she possessed no such degree of acquired knowledge or native taste and judgment, as rendered her opinion *intrinsically* of much importance. She was a daughter of Judge Will[e]s. She used to rave about Miss Wordsworth and was warmly interested in my brother—Hartley, to whom she showed substantial kindness and this feeling on her part was not short-lived but maintained with constancy. Sir G. B. was also fond of Hartley.

I meant to have added that Lady B's aged beauty, though not a beauty of mere expression but physical, did not preclude the traces of years. She looked her age, and was not what is called a specially *well preserved* woman, except that she kept her teeth which is a great point in the retaining of beauty in old age. Mrs Gillman is now very handsome in advanced life, having this advantage, so that the fine contour of her face remains unimpaired. She is Mrs Siddons in little with sparkling black eyes and a white skin. Lady B was drest picturesquely when I saw her last in widowhood, with a sort of veil head-dress.

Page 166, Mem.

S. C. [Lines 5–7 are marked in the margin.]

Page 167, Mem.

S. C. [Lines 13–26 are marked in the margin.]

Page 168, Mem.

S. C. [First paragraph is marked in the margin.]

Page 169, Mem.

S. C. [First eight lines are marked in the margin.]

Page 170, Mem.

S. C. [Lines 6–10 are marked in the margin.]

Page 176, Mem.

S. C. [Lines 3–18 are marked in the margin.]

Page 182, Mem. "Alas, alas! they may be taught, I own, more quickly to read and write under the Madras system, and to answer more readily, and perhaps with more intelligence, questions put to them, than they could have done under dame-teaching. But poetry may, with deference to the philosopher and religionist, be consulted in these matters; and I will back Shenstone's schoolmistress, by her winter fire and in her summer garden-seat, against all Dr. Bell's sour-looking teachers in petticoats that I have ever seen."

S. C. Old women ignorant themselves, generally feeble and peevish, are the worst possible teachers. How can they be good instructors who take to teaching to eke out a living, because they are incapable of any gainful occupation in other way, and take to this because the work done is less critically examined by those who pay for it than any other labour performed for hire. I do not apologize for this plain contradiction of the great man—facts publicly known having brought most thoughtful persons to one opinion on the merits or demerits rather of Dame-schoolism.

Page 183, Mem. "The old dame did not affect to make theologians or logicians; but she taught to read."

S. C. ["taught to read" is heavily underscored with comment opposite]: Did she? Slowly and often not at all.

Page 189, Mem. "Emulation, as I observed in my last letter, is the master-spring of that system. It mingles too much with all teaching, and with all learning."

S. C. The evils of emulation seem to be overstated. I have never seen any harm arise from it balanced as it is by a thousand other influences. Boys & girls generally like their rivals in pursuits of every kind. Their dislikes arise from dispathy & mutual misunderstanding and selfishness about matters of sense.

Page 191, Mem. "Hogarth understood human nature better than these professors: his picture I have not seen for many long years, but I think his last stage of cruelty is in the dissecting room."

S. C. !! The cruel wretch comes to be dissected, but did Hogarth mean by the picture to satirize surgery, and can this be a serious argument against anatomical study & practice to make perfect?

Page 200, Mem.

S. C. [Last eight lines are marked in the margin.]

Page 254, Mem. "Sound minds find their expediency in principles; unsound, their principles in expediency."

S. C. [This thought is doubly marked in the margin.]

Mem. "In fact, means, in the concerns of this life, are infinitely more important than ends."

S. C. [This thought is doubly marked in the margin.]

Page 305, Mem. "He said there was some foundation in fact, however slight, for every poem he had written of a narrative kind."

S. C. [This thought is doubly marked in the margin.]

Page 327, Mem. "These verses, it will be observed, take up the beauty long before it is matured, as one cannot but wish it may be among some of the desolations of Italy, France, and Germany."

S. C. Qy The sense—

Page 329, Mem.

S. C. [The last fourteen lines are marked in the margin.]

Page 330, *Mem.*

S. C. [First two lines are marked in the margin. The first paragraph beginning "It was Mr. Theed," etc., is marked with a cross in the margin. The first seven lines of the last paragraph are marked in the margin.]

Page 341, *Mem.* "For 'artistical' let them substitute 'artificial,' and the poetry written on this system, both at home and abroad, will be, for the most part, much better characterised."

S. C. ? [A question mark is the only comment.]

Page 355, *Mem.* One of the most gratifying circumstances of that inauguration was that he was presented for his degree by a person, whose claims on the gratitude of posterity are in many respects similar to his own.

S. C. [The last four words: "similar to his own," are underscored.] ! What would W W. have thought of this opinion from his own nephew, lightly as he esteemed of[1] the Keble Poetry. I have heard him say Watts wrote better poems than those of the Christian Year. NB

Page 359, *Mem.* Serious in aspect, tall in person, thoughtful in demeanour, unobtrusive in manner, he bore in his appearance an air of earnestness and gravity.

S. C. [The words: "tall in person," and "an air of earnestness and gravity," are underscored.] What has the tallness to do with that?

Page 383, *Mem.* "I never saw a person of your country [America], which is remarkable for cordiality, whose manner was so thoroughly cordial. . . . By the by, I heard him preach an excellent sermon in London. I believe this privilege is of modern date."

[1]Obsolete phrase; the last appearance of which recorded in N.E.D. is 1633.

S. C. [The words: "which is remarkable for cordiality," and "privilege" are underscored in the text and marked with question marks in the margin.]

Page 384, Mem. "Do you know Miss Peabody of Boston? She has just sent me, with the highest eulogy, certain essays of Mr. Emerson. Our ——— and he appear to be what the French used to call *esprits forts*."

S. C. Carlyle?[1]

Emerson's philosophy is very different from Carlyle's I believe fundamentally. Emerson appears to be an atheistic Pantheist. Not so Carlyle, who views the moral government of God in all the great events & in the general course of history.

These volumes contain a good deal of Mr W's criticisms. Yet they give a very one-sided portrait of his critical mind and conversation; because it was his habit to censure & analyse with severity the works of many of his popular contemporaries. Here you see nothing but to his courtesies to authors themselves—a polite letter to Montgomery on his Omnipresence of the Deity which I have heard him call "the omnipresence of folly & nonsense:" no depreciation of Byron, Campbell, Scott, Carlyle &c &c.

Page 386, Mem. [Footnote]. Sonnets on the Punishment of Death, . . . which were reviewed in the Quarterly, in an article ascribed to the pen of a person distinguished as a poet and an essayist.

S. C. ["ascribed" is underscored.] No longer ascribed but acknowledged by Henry Taylor

Page 390, Mem. "Poor Mr. Wade! . . . His desire to have my address must have risen, I think, from a wish to communicate with me upon the subject of Mr. Al[l]ston's valuable portrait of Coleridge. Pray tell me what has, or is likely to, become of it."

[1]A correct guess at the name left blank in the text, as the original letter reveals.

S. C. Mr W. told me that he had urged Mr Wade to leave the picture to me for my life, & to be in some public institution, Jesus Coll. or the Nat Gall. afterwards.

Page 409, Mem.

S. C. [Lines 8–16 are marked in the margin.]

Page 416, Mem. "I ought not to conclude this first portion of my letter without telling you that I have now under my roof a cousin, who some time ago was introduced, improperly, I think, she being then a child, to the notice of the public, as one of the English poetesses, in an article of the Quarterly so entitled. Her name is Emmeline Fisher, and her mother is my first cousin."

S. C. [The word "improperly" is underscored.] It is hardly worth while to notice how unfairly the writer of this review was dealt with on the subject of his notice of Miss E. F.That notice *courted* in every way, both before & after the publication of the article, cited at the same time when it was seen that the great man disapproved, an *appearance put on* of shrinking from it and annoyance at it. In an unpleasant letter I was told of the *pain* that had been given. Yet *after this*, fresh manuscripts were sent and *renewal of the "pain"* invited! Mr & Mrs W's way on this and kindred subjects was calculated to produce a sort of semi-pretense [,] something approaching to hypocrisy.

Mrs W. exclaimed when Mr W spoke of Dora's book as if she could not bear such publicity. D. would never have published but for *the money*. I am sure I would not have a daughter of mine publish *for money*, what she would not have published for the Public's sake. *After all* has not every talent possessed by any near relative of Mr W. been proclaimed—every composition worth reading been published?—even to Miss H's lines on the Redbreast? No—not the Scotch tour

Page 437, Mem. "Wordsworth made some striking remarks on Goethe in a walk on the terrace yesterday."

S. C. [The word striking is underscored.] Only to be regretted that W gave an opinion having no knowledge on the subject

Pages 441-2, Mem.

S. C. [Last three lines of page 441 and the first three lines of page 442 are marked in the margin.]

Page 453, Mem.

S. C. [Lines 13–27 are marked in the margin.]

Page 454, Mem.

S. C. [Lines 9–14 are marked in the margin.]

Page 455, Mem. "He [Wordsworth] discussed mesmerism very agreeably, stating strongly his detestation of clairvoyance."

S. C. [The words "of clairvoyance" are underscored and marked for comment; lines 4–10 are marked in the margin; "MSS." in line 13 is corrected to MS.] I am glad of this opinion having always felt thus of clairvoyance. I do not believe it, as commonly explained, at least positively and if it were true it might be used for evil—far more easily than for good. I would never subject myself to it.

Page 465, Mem. "He for God only, she for God in him."

S. C. Almost the only line in Milton that I dislike. It has ever seemed to me profane.

Page 466, Mem. "Speaking of his own prose writing, he said, that but for Coleridge's irregularity of purpose he should probably have left much more in that kind behind him. When Coleridge was proposing to publish his 'Friend,' he (Mr. Wordsworth) offered contributions. Coleridge expressed himself pleased with the offer, but said, 'I must arrange my principles for the work, and when that is done I shall be glad of your aid.' But this 'arrangement of principles' never took place."

S. C. Probably have left *much more!* As if Mr W's prose was dependent on the receptivity of "the Friend!!" In a similar spirit it was said, that the sale of the Lyrical Ballads was checked by the "Ancient Mariner," which "nobody *understood.*" "The Idiot Boy" and "the Thorn" were not generally understood at the time when "the Ancient Mariner" was unintelligible.

Mem. "On this day, as I have heard him more than once before, Mr. Wordsworth, in a way very earnest, and to me very impressive and remarkable, disclaimed all value for, and concern about, posthumous fame."

S. C. But see his Sonnet on Dante[1] &c

Page 472, Mem.

S. C. [Lines 4–14 are marked in the margin.]

Page 473, Mem.

S. C. [Lines 26–30 are marked with double lines in the margin.]

Page 477, Mem.

S. C. [Lines 4–6 are marked with double lines in the margin.]

Page 478, Mem. "Again, there is a profligacy, an inhuman sensuality, in his [Goethe's] works which is utterly revolting."

S. C. ? ? false

Mem. "I there indict him [Goethe] for wantonly outraging the sympathies of humanity."

S. C. ?

[1]See Wordsworth's *Memorials of a Tour in Italy, 1837*, Sonnet XIX, At Florence, especially the last two lines:

Bold with the thought, in reverence I sate down,
And, for a moment, filled that empty Throne.

Mem. "Yet man is essentially a moral agent, and there is that immortal and unextinguishable yearning for something pure and spiritual which will plead against these poetical sensualists as long as man remains what he is."

S. C. ?

Page 479, *Mem.* "The age of Louis XIV. was formed by the Port Royal amid the storms and thunders of the League."

S. C. ?

Mem. "Those petty courts of Germany have been injurious to its literature."

S. C. ?

Page 482, *Mem.*

S. C. [Lines 23–25 are marked with double lines in the margin.]

Page 500, *Mem.*

S. C. [At the end of Ellis Yarnall's long letter to Henry Reed.] One of the most interesting passages in the book is this contribution from Mr Yarnall, and with a touch of W's own feeling and manner about it, as I fancy. Yarnall is a very pleasing man and a good sample of that pleasing union of simplicity and frankness with intellectual refinement which belongs to the better of the educated Americans. They are most hospitable to foreign genius in heart & mind; they take it *home* to themselves right cordially & with a child like freshness of feeling and unreserve.

[On the yellow fly-leaf facing the back cover are the following notes or more likely suggestions for notes:]

56– Anecdote of the Study—already printed
66 Anecdote of L Tieck
96 Not variety—See Dr Ws judgm^{t} of the poet
110 Eccl^{e} Sketches I obj^{d} to this word
111 On Laud
116 The exager^{n} of Dover Cliff description
200 On Education—The omission of Mrs Barb
222 Notice what is said of Mrs Barbauld & the anecdote
244 Abo^{t} W Scott— A repetition
NB Offer Itineraries of Scotch journies 1833
254 Principles & Expediency—A wise letter to J.K.M.
255 Again why not the name?
267– NB Ws remark that something better may hereafte[r] be found than the Brit Constitution
279 NB To look for Donnes Sonnet
303 Who is Lord W?
327 Qy the Sense?
341 The proper Sentim^{t} of W. himself See p
383 H.[?] Taylor
390 Cs picture
403 Where to be found? Q^{s} writing
409 Excellent
417 Qy the writer?
430 Altoget[her] irrelevant & obtrusive
437 Who wrote these reminisces [Crossed out.]
438 Opin^{n} of Gothe worthless
441,2 Religious char^{r}—excellent
472,3 Critics poor— NB
474 incorrect
477 mistakes
478 Again Gothe

[Below and to the right are these briefer notes:]

Ch of Rome	143
Do	150–2
The Triad	157, 8
The Lady Beaum	163, 4
Dame Schools	182
Emulation	188
Surgical study	191
Keeble[*sic*] –	355
Tallness	359
Emerson-Montgomery	384 5
The Picture of Coleridge	390
Miss Fisher & the Quart Rev	417–8
Mesmerism–	455
Milton-Coleridge	465–6
Yarnall	500

INDEX

CORNELL STUDIES IN ENGLISH

I. A Bibliography of Thomas Gray. CLARK SUTHERLAND NORTHUP. $3.00.

II. The Influence of Horace on the Chief English Poets of the Nineteenth Century. MARY REBECCA THAYER, Ph.D. $1.00.

III. The Dramatic Records of Sir Henry Herbert, Master of the Revels. JOSEPH QUINCY ADAMS. $2.50.

IV. A Geographical Dictionary of Milton. ALLAN H. GILBERT, Ph.D. $3.50.

V. Italian Social Customs of the Sixteenth Century and their Influence on the Literatures of Europe. THOMAS FREDERICK CRANE. $6.00.

VI. The Jonson Allusion-Book, a Collection of Allusions to Ben Jonson from 1597 to 1700. JESSE FRANKLIN BRADLEY, Ph.D., and JOSEPH QUINCY ADAMS. $5.00.

VII. The Ecclesiastical Sonnets of William Wordsworth, a Critical Edition. ABBIE FINDLAY POTTS, Ph.D. $3.00.

VIII. Milton's Theory of Poetry and Fine Art; an Essay; with a Collection of Illustrative Passages from his Works. IDA LANGDON, Ph.D. $2.00.

IX. A Register of Bibliographies of the English Language and Literature. CLARK SUTHERLAND NORTHUP, with Contributions by JOSEPH QUINCY ADAMS and ANDREW KEOGH. $5.00.

X. Plays and Masques at Court during the Reigns of Elizabeth, James, and Charles. MARY SUSAN STEELE, Ph.D. $4.00.

XI. A Bibliography of the Poetics of Aristotle. LANE COOPER and ALFRED GUDEMAN. $2.00.

XII. Milton on Education; the Tractate of Education, edited with an Introduction and Notes, with Supplementary Extracts from Other Writings of Milton. OLIVER MORLEY AINSWORTH, Ph.D. $2.75.

XIII. A Dictionary of Actors and of Other Persons Associated with the Public Representation of Plays in England before 1642. EDWIN NUNGEZER, Ph.D. $5.00.

XIV. Elizabeth Gaskell. GERALD DEWITT SANDERS, Ph.D. $3.50.

XV. The Latin Poems of John Milton, edited with an Introduction, an English Translation, and Notes. WALTER MACKELLAR, Ph.D. $3.00.

XVI. Gianfrancesco Pico della Mirandola On the Imagination; the Latin Text, with an Introduction, and English Translation, and Notes. HARRY CAPLAN. $1.00.

XVII. The Poetics of Aristotle in England. MARVIN THEODORE HERRICK, Ph.D. $1.75.

XVIII. The Wits, or, Sport upon Sport. JOHN JAMES ELSON, Ph.D. $4.50.

XIX. The Lost Plays and Masques, 1500–1642. GERTRUDE MARIAN SIBLEY, Ph.D. $2.00.

XX. Goldsmith and His Booksellers. ELIZABETH EATON KENT. $1.25.

XXI. Wordsworth and Reed: The Poet's Correspondence with His American Editor, 1836–1850; and Henry Reed's Account of His Reception at Rydal Mount, London, and Elsewhere in 1854. LESLIE NATHAN BROUGHTON. $3.00.

XXII. Fielding's Theory of the Novel. FREDERICK OLDS BISSELL, JR., Ph.D. $1.00.

XXIII. The Greek Anthology in Italy to the Year 1800. JAME HUTTON. $3.00.

XXIV. Walt Whitman in England. HAROLD BLODGETT. $2.50.

XXV. Charles Kingsley. STANLEY E. BALDWIN. $2.50.

XXVI. Thomas Lodge. EDWARD ANDREWS TENNEY. $2.00.

XXVII. Sara Coleridge and Henry Reed. LESLIE NATHAN BROUGHTON. $1.50.